AF600508

THE CATHOLIC UNIVERSITY OF AMERICA
CANON LAW STUDIES
Number 94

PRESUMPTIONS OF LAW IN MARRIAGE CASES

A DISSERTATION

Submitted to the Faculty of Canon Law of the Catholic University of America in Partial Fulfillment of the Requirements for the Degree of

DOCTOR OF CANON LAW

BY

JOHN JOSEPH MANNING, A.B., J.C.L.,
Priest of the Diocese of Buffalo

THE CATHOLIC UNIVERSITY OF AMERICA
WASHINGTON, D. C.
1935

Nihil Obstat:

Clement V. Bastnagel, J.U.D.,
Censor Deputatus.

Washingtonii, D. C., die 31 maii, 1935.

Imprimatur:

+ Guillelmus Turner,
Episcopus Buffalensis.

Buffali, die 7, iunii, 1935.

TO MY MOTHER

MY FIRST TEACHER

TABLE OF CONTENTS

FOREWORD

The subject of this treatise, "Presumptions of Law," has for its foundation sound legal logic based on human experience, since a presumption is a judgment of the human intellect drawn from experience in human affairs. The legal value may be gained from the fact that only with the promulgation of the Code of Canon Law was any effort made by a legislator to establish with precision the use and application of this legal principle. Whereas, before the Code judges and authors were wont to declare when a presumption of law was in operation and how far it extended in application, the Code framed the presumptions in precise words to forbid the practice of invoking them arbitrarily.

The importance of presumptions may also be noted from the frequency of condemning accused in criminal trials on circumstantial evidence. The latter is only one phase of the use of presumptions. The possibility of a miscarriage of justice on slight evidence is most apparent. Hence, the necessity of judges competent to estimate the value of evidence and to form conclusions (presumptions) in conformity with reason, justice, and the law.

The treatise is divided into two parts, the first covering an attempt at disclosing the nature, operation, and effect of presumptions with an historical conspectus. No claim is made of an exhaustive historical research on the subject. The study is merely an attempt at disclosing the use of presumptions in the major stages of Canon Law development. In the second part a commentary has been offered on presumptions of law pertaining to matrimonial legislation. Again the treatment in the commentary was not intended to be extensive, but rather intensive to indicate the properties of the presumptions and their effectiveness when applied in marriage processes.

A conscious effort has been made to convey what the writer believes to be the present notion of *Praesumptio Iuris et de Iure*. The historical background and interpretation in this field was confused as well as confusing until the promulgation of the Code. As crystallized in the present legislation this type of presumption may be claimed as a product of ecclesiastical jurisprudence and thought, permitting as well as exacting a fairer administration of justice.

An expression of sincere gratitude is due those who assisted the writer so generously during his graduate course of studies. Eminent among those were the Most Reverend William Turner, D.D., Bishop of Buffalo and Professor Emeritus of Catholic University; the Rev. Valentine Schaaf, J.C.D., Dean of the School of Canon Law; the Rev. Louis Motry, J.C.D.; the Rev. Francis Lardone, J.U.D.; the Rev. Edward Roelker, J.C.D.; and Mr. John McDill Fox, LL.B., Dean of the School of Civil Law. The writer is indebted to the entire Faculty for its kindness, forbearance, and valuable assistance. Appreciation is also extended to the Missionary Servants of the Most Holy Trinity, to fellow priests and friends who by their consideration were a source of constant inspiration.

INTRODUCTION

Of the thirty-three titles of the Fourth Book of the Code of Canon Law, the section on procedure under the title "De Probationibus" receives more than ordinary consideration. (Canons 1747-1836.) From the moment a case is introduced in court, until the time a sentence is given, the major part of the procedure will necessarily be concerned with the proofs. Some details of the process may be neglected, technicalities overlooked may be given a sanation by an official, but proofs must be convincing. In other words, the trial fails for one party possibly because of the neglect of sufficient evidence and proof.

Now the entire purpose of court proceedings is to subject a contested matter to the judgment of one who has the authority and ability to administer the contested matter with justice. He must have the authority, otherwise the sentence will not be carried out. That he has the ability is always presumed. "Curia novit iura." M. Tullius Cicero, one of the best known of the Roman orators, who were also the advocates or lawyers of the classical period of the Republic, makes the following observation:

> Nam hoc necesse est, ut is qui causam nobis adjudicaturus sit, aut inclinatione voluntatis propendeat in nos, aut defensionis argumentis adducatur, aut animi promotione cogatur. Sed quoniam illa pars in qua rerum ipsarum explicatio ac descriptio posita est, videtur omnem huius generis quasi doctrinam continere, de ea primum loquemur.[1]

The famous orator's remarks are no less applicable to court procedure of the present day. While he was concerned principally in winning the case, nevertheless the objective was apparently the quest of justice by means of truth. To incline the mind of a third party, that is a judge, to one's allegations demands faith or credence in facts, persuasions, and arguments adduced. The more these arguments conform to truth the stronger the probability of assent from the dis-

[1] Cicero, *De Oratore,* Liber II, c. XXVII.

interested party. The value of a case presented before a judge will be no stronger than the cogency of reasons supporting the contention.

A litigious matter is either a thing or a right inherent in the thing. Consequently, the attempt made to vindicate the thing is manifested in procedure.

An accepted definition of proof among scholars of Canon Law is: "Rei dubiae seu controversae per legitima argumenta iudici facta ostensio." [2]

The first element to be observed is the demonstration in support of the claim. Secondly, the demonstration concerns a controverted matter. If it were certain, there would be no necessity for the demonstration. Third, the demonstration is made to a third party, a judge. Fourth, the demonstration is made by means of licit arguments since the judge is to be inclined to pass a just sentence by honest and rational means.[3]

The first matter under consideration, then, is the demonstration. This may be proposed in two-fold manner, artificially and naturally.[4]

In the enumeration of the species of proofs, Aristotle,[5] Cicero,[6] and M. Fabius Quintilianus mention the sources of evidence much to the same effect.[7]

The division of Cicero is apropos. He divides his proofs into two sections, first those matters that are found in the things themselves as wills, contracts, laws, decrees, responses, and the facts contributed by a client, and secondly, those consisting of the lawyer's own reasoning and arguments.[8]

[2] Roberti, *De Processibus,* (Rome, 1926), II, 24; Wernz, *Ius Decretalium,* (Prague, 1914), V, 449; Vermeersch-Creusen, *Epitome Iuris Canonici,* (3. ed., Rome, 1928), III, 62; S. B. Smith, *Elements of Ecclesiastical Law,* (5. ed., New York, 1887), II, 77; Schmalzgrueber, *Ius Ecclesiasticum,* (Romae, 1844), III, XIX, 1, 1.

[3] Wernz-Vidal, *Ius Canonicum,* (Romae, Gregoriana, 1927), VI, 374, note (2).

[4] Wernz-Vidal, *Ius Can.*, VI, 376; Jacobus, Menochius, *De Praesumptionibus,* Sumptibus Samuelis De Tournes, (Coloniae Allobrogum, 1686), I, 1, 5; Cicero, *De Oratore,* Lib. II, c. XXVII.

[5] *Rhetorica,* caput XV.

[6] *De Oratore,* Lib. II, c. XXVII.

[7] Quintilianus, *Institutio Oratoria,* Lib. V, c. II.

[8] Schmalzgrueber, *Ius Eccl.,* III, 19, 7.

The former are intrinsic and derived from the core of the case (*ex visceribus rei*), the latter are extrinsic. The time, place, and circumstances of a particular event cannot be altered. The same must be said of contracts, wills, and testimony. Still, as unchangeable as these events are, as many different conclusions might be drawn from them as there are persons interpreting these events. It is with such conclusions that we are mostly concerned, since these conclusions are termed in Canon Law praesumptions, in civil law they are called inferences. "Huc praecipue praesumptiones spectant."[9]

[9] Schmalzgrueber, *Ius Eccl.*, III, 19, 7. "An earlier term for this class (circumstantial evidence) was 'Presumptive evidence.' The distinction between 'presumption' in the sense of a mere circumstantial inference and in the sense of a rule of procedure affecting the duty of proof has in modern times led to a confusion. The term is often met with in the sense of inference as applied to probative value or ordinary circumstantial evidence, and as distinguishing it from testimonial evidence."—John Henry Wigmore, *Principles of Judicial Proof*, (2. ed., Boston, Little Brown & Co.), p. 12.

While there was occasion in Canon Law prior to the codification of 1918 to confound presumptive evidence and presumption of law, this confusion does not exist today. The distinctions are made by the law itself as written, namely *praesumptio, praesumptio hominis*, or *facti, praesumptio iuris*, and *praesumptio iuris et de iure.*. *Codex Iuris Canonici*, Lib. IV, pars I, Caput VI, *De Praesumptionibus*, Canons 1825-1828.

PART I

PRESUMPTIONS IN GENERAL

CHAPTER I

NATURE OF PRESUMPTION

The nature of a presumption is that it is an inference made in doubtful matters for the purpose of establishing the truth.

Canon 1852, §1: "Praesumptio est rei incertae probabilis coniectura; eaque alia est iuris, quae ab ipsa lege statuitur; alia hominis, quae a iudice coniicitur."

Etymologically the word presumption is derived from the Latin *prae-* meaning "before" and *sumere* meaning "to accept," that is, to accept as truth before a demonstration is advanced.[1]

In logic an inference is a conclusion drawn from two propositions or facts. Ordinarily a conclusion can be drawn from one fact or one proposition without adverting to the process of thought. But so much is certain that before a deduction is made it is known or assumed that the basis of a fact or proposition is true, established, or recognized as such in ordinary life. Otherwise, the deduction would be false.

It will be noted that the definition given uses the word "conjecture" and not "conclusion." This is not only a happy choice, but a logical one for it immediately excludes absolute certitude. It is not a wild guess, but a qualified judgment made in uncertainties. Reiffenstuel calls a presumption a belief.[2]

While an opinion may frequently conform with truth, it may also be in error. The definition meets this obstacle by the modifier 'probable.'

No one can make a judgment in the state of ignorance; the antecedents must be known. No one can make an honest and fair judgment in the state of doubt, since the judgment is suspended until the doubt is removed. However, a judgment can be made with the fear of a possible truth to the contrary.

[1] Schmalzgrueber, *Ius Eccl.,* III, XXIII, 1, #1.

[2] "Aestimatio"—Anacletus Reiffenstuel, *Ius Canonicum Universum,* (Paris, 1866), II, XXIII, 1, 2.

It is most apparent that this is not absolute certitude; the mere possibility of the contrary being true should make a prudent man hesitant to judge. Perhaps the antecedents are not well established, or the conclusion bridges over a tremendous gap, or the facts while definitely established by their nature or character permit of several, not only possible, but also probable solutions. The most probable of these opinions would constitute a real presumption. Hence, some indication or sign must precede the judgment in order to give it a foundation and reason, as in cause and effect. The cause is not an efficient cause as used in first principles or as in a system of mathematics, but is intrinsically fundamental and gives rise to a fair conclusion according to the force of the indications.

Scholars have designated these indications as signs, circumstances, "indicia," arguments, suspicions, adminicles.[8]

In general these terms can be reduced to facts, indications, or circumstances. Arguments and suspicions may in themselves be presumptions, also, the basis for further and more weighty presumptions. Adminicles are proof in their own small sphere and aid in making other proofs more conclusive especially in defective direct testimony.

In the estimation of human affairs or in judging the consequences of free agents it is seldom that more than human certitude can be obtained. To all practical purposes this is all that is demanded. Judicial matters always involve human beings. It is different when drawing conclusions from laws in physics. Thus, if a pencil falls to the ground the law of gravity is in operation. Experience teaches that fire burns, ice cools, water flows down hill, etc., but in dealing with the subtleties of free will there is no conclusive rule of action without exception, so that given certain conditions there will always follow one definite result. The conclusions will always be in the realm of probabilities.

Now, the object of every court process is justice via truth, and the attempts made to establish the truth will be the strongest means available.

Philosophers teach that there are three distinct types of certitude, metaphysical, physical, and moral. Metaphysical certitude concerns truths to which assent is given principally in the abstract. It is the

[8] Menochius, *De Praesumptionibus,* I, 7.

strongest type of certitude a human being may possess, for example, one's own existence.

Physical certitude concerns for the most part the concrete, as for example, the effects of physical laws, or one's own sensations based on experience with these physical laws.

Moral certitude, while it is the weakest of the three, is the one most frequently in use. It is based on authority or testimony. The authority may be the word or experience of another commuted to us or it may be one's own personal and individual experience, or experience with other men.[4]

Another essential factor must be considered in the nature of presumption, namely, great likelihood. On the whole, an ordinary presumption is the same as an opinion, since the conclusion is always made with a fear of doubt that the contrary may be true.[5]

While there is nothing in the essence and qualities of the antecedents to force the mind to assent that an opinion is absolute truth, the presumption is regarded as truth.

The nature of a presumption then, is not an apodictical truth, or one based on the laws of physical certainty, but one that does grant moral certainty. It is an approach to the absolute truth. It is the judgment based on a careful analysis of evidence that by exclusion of prudent fear of its being untrue the conclusion arrived at is accepted as true. It is an interpretation of facts and circumstances that is truthlike, in harmony with reality, since the predicate of every opinion is the word "probable." [6]

In the word inference there is present an indication of a logical deduction. The same is true of the word "praesumptio" in so far as the process of deduction is omitted and the truth accepted without the process of proof. We infer from antecedents. In fact, the value of the inference depends on the antecedents. Menochius, in his monumental work on *Presumptions* includes the words *coniecturae, signa,* and *indicia* in the title.

[4] P. Coffey, *The Science of Logic,* (2nd Impression, Longmans, Green and Co., London-New York, 1918), II, 214.

[5] S. D'Angelo, *Ius Digestorum,* (Romae, 1927), I, 488.

[6] John Henry Cardinal Newman, *Grammar of Assent,* (London, Longmans Green & Co., 1903) p. 60.

Some of the scholars of his time were prone to identify these antecedents, "indicia," with the presumptions themselves.[7] Like many of his contemporaries he also confounds effects in nature with presumptions classifying them as necessary presumptions and on some occasions *praesumptiones iuris et de iure.*[8]

If the signs are the antecedents, they cannot be the presumptions themselves, but preferably part of the whole, not the cause but the basis for the mental superstructure, not necessary indications, but probable, not indicative of the absolute truth, but the truth-like.

Reduced to basic reasoning the apprehension of facts or events and the conclusions drawn from them are simply acts of the intellect. "Nihil est in intellectu, quod prius non fuerit in sensu."

The process is syllogistic, since in conjunction with these particular events the mind is unconsciously using moral universals.[9] The facts, the signs, the circumstances, in general the indications are the starting point always in a presumption. They may be defined as "any significant mark aiding in discovering the truth of doubtful event."[10] By reason of association with the conclusion these indications may be conclusive or doubtful, proximate or remote. A further division usually advanced by authors, and one which seems more reasonable, is slight, serious, or grave indications.[11]

While this division is more or less a matter of individual apprehension and evaluation of the indications it, nevertheless, has some value.

The particular signs examined singly may be of no value in even raising a hazy suspicion in reference to an event. But by collating the circumstances and weaving them together strand for strand in proper relation it is possible to construct from a maze, a probable solution, a veritable "Ex pede Herculem."

[7] Menochius, *De Praesumptionibus,* I, 7.

[8] Menochius, *De Praesumptionibus* I, 7, 37 & 38.

[9] Coffey: *The Science of Logic,* I, 393 sqq.; II, 217; *Summa Theologica,* 2a, 2ae, Quaest. 2, Art. 1.

[10] Schmalzgrueber, *Ius Eccl.* III, XXIII, 1, 20; Menochius, *De Praesumptionibus,* I, 7, 20; Paul Hinschius, *Kirchenrecht,* (Berlin, 1897), vol., 6^1, 106.

[11] Schmalzgrueber, *Ius Eccl.,* III, XXIII, 1, 20; Reiffenstuel, *Ius Can. Univ.,* II, XXIII, 1, 12.

The fewer the signs the more difficult it is to ascertain the truth. Consequently, the conclusion to be drawn must be made from a consideration of right and equity. Only a prudent unbiased and disinterested man of tempered mature experience can estimate the weight of circumstances fairly lest any injustice be committed. The signs when once established remain as they are, simply signs. The material evidence in a blood-stained shirt indicates no more than that this shirt has these blood stains on it. But the interrelation of facts may be so close and of such description as to dove-tail part for part like the many-cornered and vari-colored sections of a picture puzzle.[12]

It will be observed later that the so-called *praesumptiones hominis* receive their force and value from the indications, signs, and circumstances from which they have been drawn.

[12] Wigmore, *Principles of Judicial Proof,* p. 97; Menochius, *De Arbitriis Iudicum,* Lib. II, Cas. 279, 1-4; Reiffenstuel, *Ius Can. Univ.,* II, XXIII, 1, 17.

CHAPTER II

PRAESUMPTIO HOMINIS

To make a judgment is the prerogative of the human intellect and, since presumptions are the result of mental operations, they must have their origin in man. Facts in a trial do not infer of themselves, but indicate inferences.

In every use of the principle of evidence there is some basic reason for admitting it as such. In the testimony of a witness his ability to relate with consistent truthfulness is often taken for granted.[1] Still from the wording of Canon 1756 it might better be stated that the witnesses, the documents, and material offered as evidence enjoy a presumption, in so far as it is required to show the irrelevancy or incredibility rather than its lack of probative value, before the testimony presented can be disqualified.

The value of a narration of facts by a witness is estimated by the corroboration of other testimonies in the form of witnesses, documents, facts, and circumstances attendant upon the issue. Also, besides the narration there is the veracity of the individual to be considered.

Now in each of these instances a natural presumption is being employed. Frequently, it can be demonstrated that a witness does not know the entire case, but the information given may serve as adminicular proof, at least to a concomitant fact or circumstance. With reference to documents, especially public, once they are sealed by a representative of authority, they become direct evidence. But, the entire value of the proofs is ultimately founded on the presumption that the witness is telling the truth and that the documents are genuine. Until the contrary is demonstrated the testimony is accepted as truth. Consequently, it must be admitted that there is another element in the force of proof that is not so apparent as the proof itself. Also, it

[1] Canon 1756; Wernz-Vidal, *Ius Can.*, VI, 402; Hinschius, *Kirchenrecht*, 6[1], p. 105.

must be said that in the absence of direct testimony, facts and circumstances connected with an event, whether antecedent or subsequent are not totally destitute of value in aiding the intellect to form conclusions. In procedure, these matters could not be given as direct evidence. In themselves they are mute and cannot attack or defend. But, like "Caesar's wounds," every fact and circumstance may fairly shout in accusation when all are collected and collated, so that the indications point to only one, to the exclusion of other possible solutions.

Schmalzgrueber offers as a definition of a *presumption of man*, that it is a conjecture not expressed in or based on a law, but drawn from the circumstances of the case and accepted as true until the contrary is demonstrated.[2]

Since it is not expressed in a law or rule of law it is simply the offspring of the human mind. The question naturally arises how then can a true judgment be made if the evidence is unclear, not indicative of the conclusion, not totally conformable with the facts? Again, if facts permit of so many interpretations due to their circumstances by what rule are they measured in order to obtain even probability? Thus, A is observed running from the scene of a crime. By what rule is A suspected a murderer? Again, the stolen property is found in the possession of B. Why is B believed to be a thief? A son is referred to as the heir of an estate of his father. By what norm is the son judged the legitimate heir? The answer is in the use of MORAL UNIVERSALS, namely, in the example of the murderer it is generally believed that to flee from the scene of a crime is a sign of guilt; in the case of the stolen property it is believed that the one who steals must retain the object for a reasonable time; or in the last case, that all children succeed in the estate of the parents.

There is then a normal mode of action for human beings. It cannot be called a law, nor an iron-clad rule, but an order of the normal mind in judging from antecedent experience and in applying this experience to a subsequent case. In this operation the memory and experience are tapped and the intellect forms the conclusion. Hence, because of varied experience and the total individuality of each mind

[2] Schmalzgrueber, *Ius Eccl.*, III, XXIII, 1, 4.

the conclusion in reference to another person's actions is never absolutely certain. It is only probably certain.

While a conjecture of this sort only approaches truth would it be permissible to act in such event? Experience tells us that people do. The life of the entire human race is based on probabilities. There are so many ordinary assumptions in operation in daily existence that probabilities become the guide and sometimes the rule of life. Hopes and aspirations, successes and failures, concerted and individual, public and private action all find their root in the use of probabilities, the estimation of practical certainties.[3]

Coffey, in describing the nature and use of the *Enthymeme* of Aristotle, enumerates five classes of action that call for probable assent. The class that concerns the present use of presumptions is Aristotle's syllogism from probabilities and syllogism from signs.[4] In a juridical process it amounts to the estimation of evidence, building up a proof, either in the form of a chain of evidence or viewing the accumulation of evidence as a whole.

In his chapter on Circumstantial Evidence, Professor Wigmore writes as follows: "Note that at each of these steps of [catenate] inference there is room for doubt, and that each of the inferences rests on a conclusion supposed to be reached through the preceding inference."[5] His demonstration in conveying the idea of the necessity of basing inferences only on known facts proceeds in the manner that A is based on B, B upon C, C upon D, etc. This process of proof is called by scholastics a *sorites*. It is the so-called Catenate Inference or chain evidence.

Obviously, a chain can be no stronger than its weakest link, and the ultimate inference can be no stronger than its weakest antecedent. If in each inference there is room for doubt, it is because each subsequent inference partakes or inherits as it were the weakness of the former.

[3] Coffey, *Science of Logic,* II, 264; Lepidi, *Elementa Philosophiae Christianae,* I, p. 318 apud Coffey II, p. 264, n. 1: "Tota praesens vita per probabilitatem maxime ducitur. Relationes omnes hominum in familia et in republica viventium, probabilitate fundantur. Qui scribit, qui navigat, qui militat, qui uxorem ducit, et qui leges condit, nonnisi intuitu probabilis eventus operatur."

[4] Coffey, *Science of Logic,* II, 265.

[5] Wigmore, *Principles of Judicial Proof,* p. 14.

The writer prefers to view circumstantial evidence not as a "chain," but each fact, sign, or circumstance as an independent factor in determining the conclusion. By comparison it is similar to converging the rays of light at one point by means of a prism, but the force of the combined effect will not depend upon the instrument gathering the rays (a skillful lawyer), but rather upon the combined power of the intensity of the light-rays themselves.[6]

Therefore, the intimate relation between the facts and the conclusion determines the force of the conclusion, as a general rule. The mental process suppresses the second premise or one term in the syllogism so that the deduction is valid while the process may not be so evident.

The classification previously given the *indicia* by writers gives rise to presumptions that are either light, or strong, or violent according to accepted terminology. The degrees of value have no arbitrary classification. Experience and customs of nations and the norms that influence the estimation of human conduct determine their weight.

Scholars of Roman and Canon Law of the thirteenth and following century endeavored with great pains to distinguish the *indicia* to determine when presumptions were mere suspicions, serious presumptions, or violent.[7] Their conclusions were naturally based on the jurisprudence of their time. While their decisions differ from those of the present day, it would be incorrect to say that their opinions were not well founded. In some instances their judgment was no different than that of today. At least it can be said that their attempts at arriving at the truth were actuated by motives of justice and faith.

Consequently, degrees of probability must be admitted as well as degrees of signs leading up to these probabilities. If a man is observed carrying a deadly weapon it cannot immediately be inferred that he is a criminal. He may be authorized by law to protect the general public against criminals. The presumption would be far fetched and

[6] The figures representing circumstantial evidence as a cable, or a body are also given by Professor Wigmore, *Principles of Judicial Proof*, p. 622. These figures serve the purpose of a graphic example of circumstantial evidence in all departments save one, the relation in sequence of time of the circumstance to the event.

[7] Menochius, *De Praesumptionibus*, I, 6, 7, and 14.

would amount to nothing more than a suspicion. Should a married woman be seen talking with a young man on a public thoroughfare it would be wrong to raise the cry of adultery. If the same married woman is seen frequently with men other than her husband in secluded places at late hours unescorted by another woman, there is reason to believe that she is not a faithful wife. Should it be established that John's footprints lead to the scene of the crime, that blood stains are on his clothing, that the weapon used was found in his possession, that an enmity existed between him and the victim, then the mind is forcibly urged to conclude that John is the murderer.[8]

Now in each of these cases it will be observed that the conclusion can be overthrown in spite of the fact that the inferences are valid and based on universals that lead to moral certainty. Any suspicions in the first case would be negligible unless supported by other evidence. In the second instance it could be demonstrated that the woman was in the company of her immediate relatives, as her brother. Finally, in the third case it is possible to prove that John killed his victim in self-defence. It is, also, apparent that the mind of a prudent man will be influenced by such inferences, but before he would accept these as truth he would in justice not only permit, but exact a counterproof to determine the truth. "Audiatur et altera pars." This is one of the specific qualities of a presumption of man or of fact that the judgment thus made from the facts presented is accepted as true until the contrary is demonstrated.

In this particular action of the mind the presumption becomes proof in effect. There is a difference in admitting the validity of the inference and admitting that it actually could be accepted as proof.

There is a great danger in forming a presumption, that one party may use gratuitous assertions in the attempt to force the opponent to answer all doubts even though they have no relevancy in the case at issue. No one should be forced to answer questions that are groundless. Neither is an opponent obliged to settle all matters of doubt. The general rule still holds that if the inference is drawn from established facts and circumstances and is intimately and directly connected with these facts it becomes truthlike, a verisimilitude.

[8] Schmalzgrueber, *Ius Eccl.,* III, XXIII, 5 and 6.

The only successful way to overcome a presumption is to establish the truth. Other presumptions may be set up that are more forceful and successfully overthrow those that have been made. Again, conclusions may be drawn without considering all the evidence that has been offered. And when these presumptions militate one against the other their force and strength ultimately are dependent upon the ability of the one designed to judge them.[9]

It will be noted that, since all these circumstances are to be judged only by a competent person, the classification of light, strong, and violent presumptions is practically useless. What under extenuating circumstances might be judged a definite indication of a most serious effect may turn out to be the sign of an innocent action. The sum total of all signs must be judged in their entirety in their corresponding and respective relation in order to conclude their determining value. Prejudice, influence, fear, and the will to prove a fact from circumstances may too easily color an event beyond recognition.

The vital question now arises as to the value of these inferences in court. Can a judge pass sentence from presumptions of man? The general rule advanced by authors is that in contentious cases valid presumptions of man will constitute full proof. Authors are divided on the permissibility of rendering a sentence on presumptions of fact or of man alone in criminal cases.[10]

There are four distinct opinions given on this subject. 1) The accused can be convicted or condemned on violent presumptions provided that they produce moral certainty. 2) The accused can not be convicted or condemned on violent circumstantial evidence and should be absolved because of doubt. 3) The accused is not to receive the full rigor of the law if presumptions alone point to his guilt, but the judge should inflict a milder penalty. 4) (a) If the presumptions are Iuris et de Iure, the accused should be convicted and condemned on the strength of these. (b) If the presumptions are light he should not be condemned in cases of occult crimes that by their nature would be proved only with difficulty. (c) Violent presumptions and the testimony of two unimpeachable witnesses that corroborate these

[9] Menochius, *De Arbitriis Judicum,* II, 84.

[10] S. B. Smith, *Elements,* II, 114.

presumptions would suffice for conviction or condemnation.[11] It should be noted in these opinions that the authors [12] are influenced by the jurisprudence antedating the Code, where violent presumptions were confused with presumptions of law and presumptions of law about the law. While cases involving a state of life never become *res iudicatae* and can always be reintroduced in court the presumptions invoked would not have the dire effect as if applied to criminal cases. With due respect to the opinion of so eminent a canonist as Schmalzgrueber, the temperate judgment of Saint Augustine and Innocent III is to be preferred.[13]

From the references as given in Wernz-Vidal,[14] Hinschius,[15] and Droste-Messmer,[16] the object of a criminal trial is to obtain moral certitude and with such care and circumspection that falsehood would do no violence to the accused and wickedness not replace equity. The judge should be influenced by the presumptions of the law, not by personal feelings or conjectures. From the old principle mentioned above from Roman Law the proofs must be conclusive and the accused favored.

[11] Schmalzgrueber, *Ius Can.*, III, XXIII.

[12] Schmalzgrueber, *Ius Can.*, III, XXIII, 15.

[13] St. Augustine in c. 1, C. 2, q. 1: "Nos in quemquam sententiam ferre non possumus nisi aut convictum, aut sponte confessum." Innocent III in c. 14, X, *De Praesumptionibus,* II, 23: "Propter solam suspicionem quamvis vehementem, nolumus illum de tam gravi crimine condemnari." Cf. Reiffenstuel, II, XXIII; Digest, 48, 19, 5: ". . . Sed nec de suspicionibus debere aliquem damnari, Divus Traianus Asiduo Severo rescripsit; satius enim esse, impunitum relinqui facinus nocentis, quam innocentem damnare. . . ."

[14] Wernz-Vidal, *Ius Can.*, VI, 469-470; Devoti, *Inst. Can.*, III, 9.

[15] Hinschius *Kirchenrecht,* 6^1, 108.

[16] Droste-Messmer, *Canonical Procedure in Disciplinary and Criminal Cases of Clerics,* p. 126.

CHAPTER III

PRÆSUMPTIO IURIS

Thus far, consideration has been given to the value of presumptions as an operation of the human intellect alone. There is still another source of presumptions found in the law itself. Whereas presumptions of man are drawn by a judge, the presumptions of law are drawn by the legislator. The difference between the two in the Code of Canon Law is that in presumptions of law the legislator introduces a probable result from events that frequently happen, to prevent general danger to the welfare of the community. The law-maker is making legislation, the judge is passing judgment only; the former is general, the latter particular; the legislator is conjecturing for the future; the judge is considering past acts; the law's presumption is limited in number and conditions; a judge's presumptions are innumerable. Still, there is no difference in the intellectual operation between judge and law-maker.

The real nature of the *praesumptio iuris* consists in this, that the law sets down some abstract situation as a premise. The premise may be one fact or a collection of fact and circumstances. Whenever this abstract situation or collection of facts materializes in a certain case the law states the result of the eventuality. This is not arbitrary and unreasonable on the part of the legislator. Obviously, it may be demonstrated that the law does not apply in this case in its conclusion, that the conclusion positively does not result as set forth in a legal statute. But the presumption enacted in the law still remains in spite of the fact that in the particular event it does not apply.

In drawing these conclusions the legislator is guided by universal experience which teaches that in the majority of cases this is the result of these facts and circumstances. Exceptions to this rule may arise only rarely. Consequently, the exception to the rule is permitted to be demonstrated. If it is not demonstrated, either conclusively or only doubtfully, the law will maintain its conclusion in the particular event.

Two ideas must be given particular attention in the *praesumptio iuris.* First, the foundation (antecedent facts, circumstances, indications) as specified in the law must be established. Secondly, the deduction, that is, the conclusion itself, is not demonstrated step by step as flowing from these antecedents. The law admits the gap, the mental bridge, the leap in the ratiocination. More so, the law actually authorizes the conclusion and directs the judge to cling to this conclusion without any process of proof until the adversary can prove either directly or indirectly that the presumption does not hold.

Indirectly the adversary can show that the foundation does not exist or is wanting in one of its constitutive parts to form a real foundation as required by the presumption. Directly, it can be proved that while the foundation does exist the evident truth is contrary to the presumption. An example will, perhaps, render this more obvious. Canon 88 § 3 states that those who have reached the age of seven years are presumed to have the use of reason. This is a matter of general experience throughout the world; hence, to attribute to a person imputability of acts requiring ordinary discretion the law makes the presumption that this mental capacity is present when a child has reached its seventh birthday. The presumption of law is *use of reason;* the foundation of the presumption is *seven years of existence from birth.* The attack can be made indirectly to overcome the force of the law by removing the foundation, the prop supporting the presumption, in this case the denying of or showing the lack of seven years of age. Obviously if the support is removed the superstructure, the presumption, falls. A direct attack would leave the suppositum stand, in this case the seven years, and impugn the presumption itself, in this case the age of reason; namely, it might be demonstrated that in spite of the fact that the child is seven years old it lacks discretion because it is an imbecile.

However, if neither of these attacks are successful the presumption will be adhered to by the law.

Consequently, two striking effects enjoin upon *praesumptiones iuris.* In effectiveness a legal presumption is full proof. The court is relieved of the duty of explaining its deductions; before any proofs to the contrary are advanced the presumption is fully maintained as the truth, namely, full proof; or, in facts, as soon as the foundation is completed the presumption of law is automatically present.

The second striking effect is that by its nature the presumption of law shifts the entire burden of proof onto the one opposing it. This is called a rule of procedure and is most advantageous at any stage of a trial. The law simply arrogates to one party complete immunity as to this obligation. It is an automatic effect and favors the defendant in his suit as well as the court in procedure and preponderance of evidence. By way of example, Canon 1014 contends that all marriages are presumed valid until the contrary is demonstrated. Consequently, if one of two parties should raise a doubt as to the validity of a marriage it is not the obligation of the other party to demonstrate that the marriage is valid. On the contrary, the one questioning the marriage must furnish all evidence that this marriage for some reason is not valid. There is, however, some obligation on the party who claims a presumption of law. The facts on which the presumption rests must be established in judicial manner, *i. e.,* during the process of the trial. To overthrow this presumption then, the opponent either attacks the presumption itself or the facts upon which it rests. Objections and doubts raised about the contrary of the legal deduction do not count. Real proofs must be proposed to overthrow the force of the provision of the law.

Cognizance might also be taken of the fact that nowhere does the law say that this is the evident truth. It admits that the evident truth to the contrary destroys it. Should the real truth in the course of a process become manifestly identical with the presumption, it would no longer be held as a presumption, but the truth. However, there are certain events in human existence that can never be known with certainty. The element of doubt may always show its head at least to allow the mind to incline to an opposite conclusion. It is in such situations that presumptions of law are drafted since the *bonum commune* demands safeguards *ad cavendum periculum generale.* Consequently, a presumption of law tenaciously maintained by a judge is not declaring the absolute truth of the eventuality, but the truthlike. By following the norm of greatest probability, the law enacts that in justice and of necessity this is the nearest approach to truth.

It is evident that a presumption of law may be maintained as true and a definitive sentence rendered on the strength of it unless the contrary is proved. It will also be observed that this is not a proof in itself, but only becomes a proof in effect. A party who contends that a presumption of law stands in his favor is said to have his contention founded in the law.

It was the opinion of some scholars that all violent presumptions were presumptions of law.[1] This opinion does not obtain in the legislation of today. Neither can results in nature or matters of necessary cause and effect be regarded as presumptions of law, such as smoke from a chimney means fire below, "coisse quae peperit, etc." [2] These are not conjectures, since there is no doubt possible.

Strange as it may seem, commentators on Roman Law and scholars in Canon Law of the present day have formulated their notions and definitions in much the same fashion, but their application is widely different. It is possible that these authors have been influenced by confusing opinions of the earlier jurists and writers who identified natural assumptions and the Regulae Iuris as typical presumptions of law as in the modern Code. Zallinger distinguishes between a "*presumptio iuris simplex* and *qualificata*." Among the former he places such general presumptions as "Nemo malus nisi probatur," "quivis praesumitur legitime natus." In the second classification he mentions qualities that are in the individuals or the objects by nature, as, a presumption is in favor of the possessor, a presumption of capability favors a candidate promoted.[3] He makes a third classification called "*praesumptio iuris violenta*" and mentions in this group "*matrimonium post cohabitationem plurium annorum praesumitur validum,*" and the rule for legitimacy.

Reiffenstuel, also, has a classification of "*praesumptiones naturae*" and implies that by their force they also shift the burden of proof.[4] Schmalzgrueber while he has not a similar classification applies these general presumptions almost recklessly in his "Regulae Praesump-

[1] Schmalzgrueber, *Ius Eccl.*, III, XXIII, 7. Cf. Wernz, *Ius Decretalium*, V, p. 493.

[2] Maroto, *Institutiones*, p. 223.

[3] Zallinger, *Institutiones Iuris Ecclesiatici, Ordine Decretalium*, II, p. 206-207.

[4] Reiffenstuel, *Ius Can. Univ.*, II, XXIII, 40-44.

tionum."[5] These general presumptions are better called "Moral Universals," mentioned previously. They are the underlying reasons for the probabilities of life and are used and frequently enforced, not as a presumption of law, but rather as general presumptions of nature common to all mankind.

[5] Schmalzgrueber, *Ius Eccl.,* III, XXIII, §II.

CHAPTER IV

PRAESUMPTIO IURIS ET DE IURE

A subdivision of *praesumptio iuris* made by the Code is a *praesumptio iuris et de iure.* Romanists and Canonists alike use the same terminology in references to it.

There is a wide difference of opinion among authors in attempting to present the notion of a *presumptio iuris et de iure.* All writers describe the concept by declaring its principal effect and its difference from other presumptions. Few attempt to describe its nature and most of them are not clear. The expression itself is altogether foreign to Roman Law. Donatuti and Burckhard [1] say that the term first appears as a glossa. The source is not indicated. Before attempting to discuss its nature and operation it must first be recognized that the phrase as written is not apt. It appears that some word is to be supplied, or that the particle "Et" is entirely superfluous. The omission of the "Et" would give a clearer concept. A glossa to c. 30, X, *De Sponsalibus et Matrimoniis,* IV, 2, apparently does this. Another glossa to c. Un. Title V, *Ne sede vacante aliquid innovetur,* in the *Extravagantes* of John XXII renders this canon a presumption Iuris et de Iure and confounds it with a violent presumption and a fiction of law. In this regard it would approach the Anglo-Saxon estoppel.[2]

Menochius' concept of the principle seems to confirm the idea of estoppel.[3] But this is contrary to the idea of presumption which operates only in matters of doubt.

Baldus' definition conveys the best notion of the concept and agrees with the glossa referred to in the Decretals. He says: "Haec prae-

[1] Guido Donatuti, *Le Praesumptiones Iuris in Diritto Romano,* (Perugia 1930), p. 6; Burckhard, *Die zivilistischen Praesumptionen,* (Weimar, 1866), p. 11.

[2] Charles P. Sherman, *Roman Law in the Modern World,* (New York, Baker, Voorhis & Co., 1924), II, 417; cf. C. 7, 65, 2; cf. Infra, p. 44.

[3] Menochius, *De Praesumptionibus,* I, 3, 13: "Lex enim ita praesumit ut verum illud esse statuat, contrariumque probari non posse decernat. Nam legis auctoritas hoc certum esse facit. Et ob id congruo nomine fidei certitudo, non ab evidentia rei, non a ratione ducta, sed ab auctoritate credibile appellatur."

sumptio iuris dicitur, quia lege introducta est: Et de iure, quia super tali praesumptione lex inducit firmum ius et habet eam pro veritate."[4] Voet in his commentary on the Digest records the same thought: "Praesumptionem juris and de jure appellant interpretes, quoties jus praesumit aliquid, ac super eo praesumpto disponit, nec admittit in contrarium probationem."[5] Why the glossator called this principle *"iuris et canonis"* is not declared, but it may be conjectured that the thought to be inferred would be that by natural law (Ius) a presumption is introduced and over and above and in support of this presumption of the natural law a human law is drafted giving it double force. It is a retroactive force. It becomes necessarily a presumption of law about the law, a sanction added by the legislator to a legal presumption. In other words the law presumes and legislates at one and the same time, but the legislation makes the presumption a law.

The concept of this presumption differs, also, from that of the simple presumption of law in the form of rebuttal it allows. Where a *praesumptio iuris* permits a direct or indirect proof to the contrary, a *praesumptio iuris et de iure* permits only indirect proof, that is, overthrowing the facts or the foundation on which this presumption rests.

Evidently, the reason for the confusion among writers is due to the fact that formerly practically no proof was permitted to the contrary. Another very apparent reason was that the law was not clearly stated. That is to say, formerly there was jurisprudence, and the application of the principles of law, whereas, today, there is positive legislation, the active application of the law itself.[5a]

Canon 1825, § 1, states first, the nature of a presumption, and secondly, the subdivision of law and of man. It further enumerates in no uncertain terms the sources of both, namely, that a presumption of man is a conjecture of the judge, and that a presumption of law is one that is effected by the law. Canon 1828 explicitly mentions that a judge may not form a presumption of law, but only a presumption of man under the usual conditions.

[4] Cf. Menochius, *De Praesumptionibus*, I, 3, 18.

[5] Joannes Voet, *Commentarium ad Pandectas,* (5 ed., Bassani, Venice, 1827), XXII, III, 16.

[5a] Canon 1825. §1. Praesumptio est rei incertae probabilis coniectura; eaque alia est iuris, quae ab ipsa lege statuitur; alia hominis, quae a iudice coniicitur.

The wording of the Canon 1828 "Praesumptiones, quae non statuuntur a iure" refers undoubtedly only to the opposite of presumptions of law, namely, presumptions of man since only two kinds are mentioned in Canon 1825. Another essential difference between *praesumptio iuris et de iure* and *praesumptio iuris* lies in this, that the former concerns only past acts.[6]

In considering the nature of a *praesumptio iuris et de iure* the notion of a simple *praesumptio iuris* can not be lost sight of. Whether in Civil or Canon Law the wording of the *praesumptio iuris* is more or less the same. A provision is usually made to permit the contrary to be proved with the expressions "nisi contrarium probetur," [7] or "nisi evidentibus argumentis contrarium probetur," [8] or "quod si non evidenter apparuit." [9] This provision is absent in the notion of a *"res iudicata"* which is mentioned in the Code expressly as a *praesumptio iuris et de iure.*

Now a *res iudicata* or judged matter has a two-fold meaning, 1) the contested matter, or the case, and 2) the judicial sentence. Thus, after two conformable sentences have been given the case becomes settled. But among canonists the common interpretation concerns the sentence. This becomes a *res indicata* when after sentence is passed the appeal is neglected or if appeal is made (*coram iudice a quo*) the case is not pursued by the appellant in the higher court (*coram iudice ad quem*).[10]

The purpose of an appeal is to obtain justice by calling on a higher authority when the party against whom the decision was given contends injury.[11]

If this same party, however, does not appeal within the specified time, the court presumes that he has renounced his right and has conceded that justice was administered in the first instance. To prevent such cases from being re-introduced and by repeated appeals avoid the fulfillment of the sentence to the injury of the successful

[6] Menochius, *De Praesumptionibus,* I, 3, 23.

[7] Canon 1536.

[8] Canon 1115.

[9] D. 23, 3, 57.

[10] Schmalzgrueber, *Ius Eccl.,* III, XXVII, 62; Wernz-Vidal, *Ius Canonicum,* VI, p. 62.

[11] Canon 1879.

party the law looks upon this case as finished, "judged," and will not permit the case to be brought into court again except in a case of manifest injustice.

In a *res iudicata* there is no ordinary *remedium* allowed against the *sententia,* as appeal, or a *querela nullitatis*. An extraordinary remedy may be taken against a sentence by a *restitutio in integrum,* but this is only permitted in certain cases. Canon 1905 mentions the exceptions: 1) when it is demonstrated that the documents on which the sentence rests were false; 2) when documents are discovered which prove new facts and demand a contrary peremptory decision; 3) when the sentence was pronounced because of deceit of one party to the detriment of the other; 4) when a prescript of law had been evidently neglected.

In these four exceptions it will be noticed that there is no direct attack made on the *res iudicata* itself, but on its foundation. The attack then is indirect, or in other words the *sententia* that has become a *res iudicata* is immune to direct attack. In the *praesumptio iuris* the legislator makes a deduction from antecedents and maintains the conclusion thus made whenever the antecedents materialize, until the contrary is demonstrated. In the *res iudicata* the same operation takes place, but the opportunity to show the contrary directly is excluded. The antecedent is the procedure which has been conducted as prescribed by law. But should this sentence become a *res iudicata* the legislator throws a guard around the actual adjudication and establishes it as a law in this particular instance to protect it. That which led up to the sententia is not so guarded, but is left open to attack. Experience demands that there be final adjudication of matters contested with few exceptions. The legislator admits, also, that there is a slight possibility of the sentence being reversed or unjust, since human beings engaged in the process are the agents and human relations are being administered with moral certitude only.

In this event two presumptions are in operation. One favors the judge of the first instance in so far as the law presumes that the trial was conducted correctly and the sentence given on the strength of the evidence in strict justice and fairness.[12]

If no appeal is made the law again presumes that the sentence was just by tacit admission of the condemned party, and immediately goes

[12] Menochius, *De Praesumptionibus,* II, 67, 1-6.

into effect. This is the "praesumptio iuris et canonis, sive legis, sive de iure" mentioned by the Glossator.[13] The effect cannot be directly impeached. To show indirectly that the arguments, or documents, or testimonies did not warrant such a sentence is permitted, but the *res iudicata* itself cannot be attacked. It is presumed conclusively by law to be true and just and until the sentence is reversed the *res iudicata* is accepted as truth.[14] The only canon in the entire Code that is so mentioned and to which can be applied this concept of *praesumptio iuris et de iure* is Canon 1904.

The index to the Gasparri edition of the Code mentions both Canons 1904 and 1972 as specimens of *praesumptiones iuris et de iure.* Now the index to the Code has no legislative or binding force. Canon 1972 itself does not say that it is a *praesumptio iuris et de iure.* Coronata's opinion is much to the point.

> "Sunt qui hunc canonem intelligunt quasi in eo statuatur validitas matrimonii post mortem unius coniugis praesumptione iuris et de iure; at Codex id non dicit; dicit tantummodo non admitti probationem nisi incidenter proponatur quaestio seu causa. At si quaestio incidens oriatur de valore matrimonii, in quaestione, e.g., de hereditate, admitti potest et probatio directa; nec enim in quaestionibus incidentibus probationes directae exclusae sunt." [15]

A source to this canon states that such an accusation would be *"incongruum."* [16] It seems more correct to state that the legislator has inserted this Canon 1972 only as a prohibition. It has the effect of the Anglo-Saxon estoppel, based apparently on the principle "De mortuis nil nisi bonum." However, because it may be necessary indirectly to investigate a marriage dissolved by death of one or both parties to determine legitimacy or succession the law permits an investigation, or an incidental attack on an otherwise closed affair.

[13] Cf. *Decretales* D. Gregorii Papae IX, Suae Integretati una *cum Glossis* restitutae, (Romae, 1582), Glossa ad c. 30, X, *De Sponsalibus et Matrimoniis,* IV, 2. Cf. Infra, p. 44.

[14] D. I, 5, 25; 50, 17, 207; cc. 13, 15, 17, X, *De Sententia et Re Iudicata,* II, 27; Canon 1904, §1; Schmalzgrueber, *Ius Eccl.,* III, 27, 62.

[15] A Coronata, *Institutiones Iuris Canonici,* (Taurini, 1933), III, 425.

[16] C. 7 and 11, X, *Qui filii sint legitimi,* IV, 17.

In the first Canon of this title *De Praesumptionibus* the legislator has settled difficulties in matters of jurisprudence existing since the beginning of Church legislation. In this particular concept of *praesumptio iuris et de iure* there is an entirely new product of ecclesiastical legislation. While there are preceptive and prohibitive laws in the Code of Canon Law, there are no irrebuttable inferences, so called rules of law, that permit of no proof to the contrary. Canon 1904 § 1, ordains that a res iudicata by reason of a *praesumptio iuris et de iure* is held as true and cannot be directly impugned.

CHAPTER V

FICTION OF LAW

A presumption of law might be so laid down by law as to be easily mistaken for a complete fiction. While the effect produced by either may be the same (presumed legitimacy and legitimation) the two principles are widely different in concept.

A fiction of law is a legal assumption induced by the law to produce an effect in equity conformable with justice, when a matter is possible but absolutely untrue.[1]

The definition of Alciatus is to the point. He says: "Fictio est legis adversus veritatem in re possibili ex justa causa dispositio." [2] Thus, a child conceived may be considered born in matters of heredity; a canon must wear the vesture of his office in choir, otherwise, be considered absent; a canon legitimately absent from choir for the evident service of the Church is considered present;[3] an invalid marriage may be given a sanation and enjoy canonical effects dating from the beginning of the marriage.[4]

The consideration granted by the law supposes the truth to what is objectively false, but, nevertheless, fair and just by nature.[5]

In other words it is the positive assertion of a matter morally and physically possible, contrary to the known truth. The following rule sums up the differences between presumptions and fictions of law in both nature and effect:

> Supra id, quod est certum, fingitur: super incerto praesumitur.[6]

[1] Angelus apud Menochius, *De Praesumptionibus*, I, 8, 7. The same given by Schmalzgrueber, *Ius Eccl.*, III, XXIII, 3, though the source is not mentioned.

[2] Alciatus, *Parergon Iuris* 6, I, 6, apud Reiffenstuel, *Ius Can. Univ.*, II, 176.

[3] Canon 409.

[4] Canon 1138, §1.

[5] Gommarus Michiels, *Normae Generales Iuris Canonici*, (Lublin, Polonia, 1929), I, p. 342.

[6] Glossa to Code of Justinian, V, 13, Lex un. § 13.

Hence, a presumption is applied in doubtful matters, a fiction of law to known facts; a presumption is a probable truth, a fiction is contrary to the truth; a presumption is used in reference to facts, a fiction in matter of fact and of rights; a presumption permits of direct and indirect proof to the contrary, a fiction permits of no proof; a presumption is a type of proof at least in effect, a fiction is no proof; a presumption can be of man or of law, a fiction is only of law; presumptions can militate against each other, fictions can not; many presumptions may concur, fictions can not; presumptions can be extended from person to person, fictions can not.[7]

[7] Cf. Maroto, *Institutiones,* I, p. 226 (Romae 1921); Renard, *Le Droit, la Justice et la Volonté,* (Paris, 1924) p. 137, n. 2; Geny, *Science et Technique en droit privé positif,* (Paris, 1921) III, p. 261.

CHAPTER VI

HISTORY OF PRESUMPTIONS

It is almost impossible to give an adequate and exhaustive history of presumptions of law. Since an ordinary presumption is an operation of the mind it must go back to the origin of mankind. There are ordinary presumptions of fact in the Bible. The famous case is the one presented to King Solomon[1] where both women claimed the one living child. When he decided that the living child should be divided in two, one of the women preferred that the child's life be spared. Solomon concluded that she was the mother of the child because of the general presumption that all mothers love their children and do not wish them harmed. There is another general presumption set up by Solomon in the Proverbs.[2]

ART. 1

ROMAN LAW—CLASSICAL PERIOD

In the field of Roman Law the problem is rife with difficulties due to the fact that the original sources are not known and secondly, on account of the Justinian interpolations. In regard to the latter the opinion of Gradenwitz must be considered.[3] It is his contention that presumptions of law (*praesumptiones iuris*) were a Justinian invention. This is also the doctrine of Ferrini.[4]

D'Angelo[5] quotes Scialoia[6] who holds a milder view, that is, that presumptions of man existed in ancient procedure and that the pre-

[1] I Kings, III, 24.

[2] Proverbs, XXX, 18 and 19; XXVI, 18 and 19.

[3] Zeitschrift der Savigny Stiftung, *Romanistische Abteilung, Interpolationen in den Pandekten* von Herrn Dr. Otto Gradenwitz, 7, pp. 45-84.

[4] C. Ferrini, *"Le presunzioni in dir. rom.,"* RISG, XIX, (1893), p. 258.

[5] D'Angelo, *Ius Digestorum,* (Romae, 1927), Pars I, p. 488-489.

[6] *Procedura Civ. Rom.,* p. 439.

sumptions of law developed in the time of Justinian from the classical forms of presumptions of man in force at that time.

In giving his excellent criticism of the text of interpolations it seems that Gradenwitz carries his claim beyond the historical discovery into the field of dogmatic interpretation in so far as he apparently concludes that presumptions of law were arrived at through Byzantine influence. It is highly possible that this eminent scholar through the impetus of his discovery should be led to believe that the interpolations are purely Justinian inventions instead of changes of expression without affecting the intention of the law. Furthermore, his investigations are based on research only in those texts in which the words "praesumptio" and "praesumere" appear. It might be demonstrated that a presumption of law existed and that Justinian simply framed the law with greater precision. Today Roman law, as in the Corpus Iuris Civilis, in its interpretation is known primarily through the study of the glossa and the glossators. In many cases not only their expressions but their concepts differ. There is wide deviation from the concept of presumption as proposed in the Code of Canon Law. Before attempting to demonstrate any development, it is necessary to discover the properties of presumptions first.

Professor Guido Donatuti[7] mentions in his study five distinct characteristics of presumptions of law as they exist in the sources, 1) A presumption of law is a judicial principle. 2) A presumption of law is a rule of procedure. 3) A presumption is proof of a fact in matters of doubt. 4) A presumption of law permits a rebuttal. 5) A presumption of law may refer to an interior element, such as a presumed act of the will.

The texts that he adduces in support of his claim are taken from the Digest and the Code of the Corpus Iuris Civilis. The authors of the texts of the Digest were Roman jurists. Now, obviously these jurists were not legislators. But while their duty was simply to offer opinions on the interpretation of law,[8] their decisions contributed in no small manner to the development of jurisprudence. The *senatusconsulta* were not laws but became equivalent to such towards the

[7] Donatuti, *Le Praesumptiones iuris in diritto Romano,* p. 3.

[8] Sherman, *Roman Law in the Modern World,* (2 ed., New Haven Law Book Co., New Haven, Conn., U. S. A., 1922), I, 45.

close of the Republic.[9] Consequently, in view of the equity of Roman Law and the high regard in which the jurists' opinions were held it might be concluded with good reason that their judicial opinions had developed into juridical maxims. To have presumptions of law it would have been necessary to introduce them actually into the law. However, it is difficult to say that they were anything more than presumptions of man (*praesumptiones hominis*), but, in effect *praesumptiones iuris*.

In Digest 22, 5, 3, there is the famous excerpt of a rescript given by Hadrian to a certain Valerius Verus on the evaluation of testimony and general suggestions on how to ascertain the truth.

> D. 22, 5, 3, § 2. Callistratus libro IV. de Cognitionibus. ". . . Eiusdem quoque Principis extat Rescriptum ad Valerium Verum de excutienda fide testium in haec verba: Quae argumenta ad quem modum probandae cuique rei sufficiant, nullo certo modo satis definiri potest, sicut semper, ita saepe sine publicis monumentis cuiusque rei veritas deprehenditur, alias numerus testium, alias dignitas et auctoritas, alias veluti consentiens fama confirmat rei, de qua quaeritur, fidem. Hoc ergo solum tibi rescribere possum summatim, non utique ad unam probationis speciem cognitionem statim alligari debere, sed ex sententia animi tui te aestimare oportere, quid aut credas, aut parum probatum tibi opineris."

It is evident from this fragment that the judge is to form conclusions drawn from facts, although the very mention of rendering decisions in accordance with presumptions is omitted.[10] Again, D. 5, 1, 79, 1 from Ulpian (and, hence, at a later period) says that the judges are to be informed on the matters of the law by the Praesides.

> D. 5, 1, 79, § 1. Ulpianus libro V. de officio Proconsulis. Iudicibus de iure dubitantibus Praesides respondere solent, de facto consulentibus non debent Praesides consilium impertire, verum iubere eos, prout religio suggerit, sententiam proferre; haec enim res nonnunquam infamat materiam gratiae vel ambitionis tribuit.

[9] Amos, (London, 1883), *Roman Civil Law*, p. 73.

[10] Cf. Cicero, *De Oratore*, Lib. II, Caput 49 and 50.

This was apparently the motive behind the advice of Hadrian in the fragment quoted. If the witnesses were allowed to appear freely and testify even as in the formulary procedure, certainly there was room for the judge to make presumptions.[11]

That this same purpose of judging matters of doubt with fairness and justice influenced the later period may be well understood from the famous Praesumptio Muciana.[12] The writings and legal mind of the great jurist Scaevola showed its influence on the law as evidenced in this particular fragment.

> D. 24, 1, 51. Pomponius libro V. ad Quintum Mucium. Quintus Mucius ait, quum in controversiam venit, unde ad mulierem quid pervenerit, et verius, et honestius est, quod non demonstratur, unde habeat, existimari, a viro, aut qui in potestate eius esset, ad eam pervenisse. Evitandi autem turpis quaestus gratia circa uxorem hoc videtur Quintus probasse.

The expression "verius et honestius" suggests equity, but the use of "existimare" and "quod non demonstratur" intimates a real presumption. That there was a real development into a precise presumption of law may be gathered from a fragment of later date (229 A. D.), in Code 5, 16, 6, 1. Here, also, the use of "veteres iuris auctores . . . credidissent" intimates that in earlier jurisprudence the same rule was applied in similar cases and that there was at least a tendency for this practice to form itself into a set maxim and later a juridical rule.[13]

Art. 2

THE POST CLASSICAL LAW

It is the common opinion of authors that the presumptions of law were not only established, but arose during the Post-classical Period, since it was at this time that the jurists' opinions had crystalized into laws. Also, the judge was making his opinions from

[11] Windsheid-Kipp, *Lehrbuch des Pandektenrechts* (9 ed., Frankfurt am Main, 1906), § 509, 36.

[12] Sherman, *Roman Law in the Modern World,* I, 47, "Scaevola."

[13] Donatuti, *Les Praesumptiones Iuris,* p. 21.

the principles of very likelihood based on the estimation of the value of proof in established facts, and from the jurists' conclusions.[1]

The progress then would be somewhat as follows: When cases of doubt arose before the post-classical period, the matters in question whether of law or of fact were presented to the jurists for study. The jurists formed opinions to settle the cases and since these were but private judgments in each individual case they were only *presumptiones hominis*. With these they instructed the judge in the exercise of the law and thereby put their opinions into effect in a juridical manner. Consequently, in the post-classical era these opinions had acquired legal value and became rules of procedure.[2] A comparison of the laws in Digest 34, 5, 9, pars. 1 and 4, dicloses this progress. The case is one of establishing prior death when father and son die at the same time and it is impossible to ascertain who died first. From the fragment of Hadrian it seems quite evident that this presumption of law did not exist in the classical era, but became a fully established working principle at the time of Tryphoninus (died after 213 A. D.). That it was necessary to establish a presumption of law at this particular time may be concluded by reason of the fact that the position of the pater-familias was weakening.

Another example of this gradual development may be noticed in connection with *fideicommissa* (trusts). The general rule for interpreting the "voluntas" in a trust is given in Code 6, 42, 16.

> Code 6, 42, 16: Sane quoniam in fideicommissis voluntas magis, quam verba plerumque intuenda sunt, si quas pro rei veritate præterea probationes habes, ad commendandam hanc patris voluntatem, quam fuisse asseveras, apud præsidem experiri non vetaris.

This particular constitution dates back to 283 A. D. The development in the matter of the "voluntas" was from equity to a presumption of man to a presumption of law.

In order to solve ambiguities in substitutions in testaments a simple presumption of man was employed as in Digest 34, 2, 18. Here

[1] Kipp, *Geschichte der Quellen*, IV, III; Krueger, *Geschichte der Quellen*, II, 125; Bonfante, *Storia*, 1, 377.

[2] Sherman, *Roman Law in the Modern World*, I, p. 97.

the jurist Scævola apparently interpreted the very likely intention of the testator.[3]

Practically the same development took place in consideration of the dowry given in Roman marriages. In Digest 2, 14, 7, 12, Ulpian *Ad Edictum* ventures the opinion that from the stipulation an action may arise. To settle the ambiguity of the stipulation it would be necessary to understand the will of both parties to the contract. A settlement of such an action before the judge would constitute a simple presumption of man which by repetition in similar cases would set a precedent so that this presumption would subsequently be transformed into a presumption of law.[4]

It can hardly be doubted that the natural presumption of legitimacy was not in use before the Codification.[5] Since it is of such importance in human affairs it must have been a genuine presumption of law in full operation. As to the wording of the law itself Gaius seems to infer that it was an accepted principle. Gaius Institutes (D. 1, 6, 3).

> "Item in potestate nostra sunt liberi nostri, quos ex iustis nuptiis procreaverimus."

Paulus later gave a response in which he framed the law with greater precision, still using the term "iustæ nuptiæ."

> D. 1, 5, 12, "Paulus libro XIX. Responsorum.—Septimo mense nasci perfectum partum iam receptum est propter auctoritatem doctissimi viri Hippocratis; et ideo credendum est, eum, qui ex iustis nuptiis septimo mense natus est, iustum filium esse."

The foundation for this presumption is placed in the teaching of Hippocrates, the so-called father of medicine, who lived in the fourth century before Christ. The same doctrine is invoked again in D. 38, 16, 3, 11:

> Ulpianus ad Sabinum:
> "Post decem menses mortis natus non admittetur ad legitimam hereditatem. §12, De eo autem, qui centesimo

[3] Gradenwitz, *Interpolationen,* 200; D. 2, 14, 7, 12.

[4] D. 23, 3, 64.

[5] D. 2, 4, 5: ". . . pater est, quem nuptiae demonstrant."

octogesimo secundo die natus est, Hippocrates scripsit, et Divus Pius pontificibus rescripsit, iusto tempore videri natum, nec videri in servitute conceptum, quum mater ipsius ante centesimum octogesimum secundum diem esset manumissa."

Still another fragment of Ulpian ad Sabinum in Digest 1, 6, 6, traces the same thought to Scævola. The law is exceptionally well written with clarity and precision.

"Filium eum definimus, qui ex viro et uxore eius nascitur. Sed si fingamus abfuisse maritum,. verbi gratia per decennium, reversum anniculum invenisse in domo sua, placet nobis Iuliani sententia, hunc non esse mariti filium. Non tamen ferendum Iulianus ait eum, qui cum uxore sua assidue moratus nolit filium agnoscere, quasi non suum. Sed mihi videtur, quod et Scævola probat, si constet maritum aliquamdiu cum uxore non concubuisse infirmitate interveniente vel alia causa, vel si ex valetudine paterfamilias fuit, ut generare non possit, hunc, qui in domo natus est, licet vicinis scientibus, filium non esse."

Art. 3

JUSTINIAN LAW

In this period, the time of Codification, presumptions in every degree were well determined by the law, as is very evident from Book XXII, Title 3 of the Digest and Book IV, Title 19 of the Code. The phrasing in Greek and the use of *πρόληψις* indicates not only a presumption in general but also a proof in doubtful matters.[1] Even the terminology had crystalized so far as to use the term præsumptio

[1] πρσληψις—1) a preconception, 2) a previous notion or conception;

προλαμβσνω—II, 5—to anticipate the event; prejudge.—Lidell & Scott; *Greek English Lexicon,* (8 ed., New York, 1897).

πρσληψις—Anticipatio, Occupacio, Praesumpcio.

Caroli Labbaei *Glossaria Graeco-Latina et Latino-Graeca* (London, 1816-1826), p. 145.

iuris in the text.[2] Donatuti and Gradenwitz[3] both concede that the presumptions of law originated with the Compilations since the variations betray themselves in the texts. They believe that such expressions as "quod præsumptum esse debet" and "nisi evidenter approbetur in contrarium" show where the legislator placed his additions to the original jurists' opinions.[4] The writer feels too incompetent to settle this famous question which, also, involves the divergence of viewpoints of the two schools of thought as to the influence of Byzantine thought or the lack of it on the Justinian legislation.

Suffice it to say, that from the context of the fragments themselves and the title in Digest 22, 3, *De Probationibus et Præsumptionibus,* there is little room for doubt that the two outstanding characteristics of Præsumptiones Iuris, namely, a conjecture in a doubtful matter and a conjecture of the law as proof in matters of doubt were conclusively established and active working juridical principles at the time of Justinian.

Art. III

PRESUMPTIONS IN CANON LAW—GRATIAN

After the edict of Milan was promulagted by Constantine in 313 A. D., it was impossible for the Roman Law to remain immune to the influence of Christianity.[1] The Church acting within her own sphere soon brought into the legislation necessary changes, as for instance, in matrimony. Since Christ had raised the conjugal life to the dignity of a sacrament and because of the importance and public character of marriage to the State, the campaign of the Church easily made itself known in legislation against divorce and concubinage.[2] In the Code rape becomes a capital crime.[3] Equity, while a substantial element of Roman Law became *humanitas, benignitas,*

[2] Bas. 11, 1, 17; 22, 1, 25.

[3] Donatuti, *Le Praesumptiones Iuris,* p. 66; Gradenwitz, *Interpolationen,* 204.

[4] Cf. D. 32, 33, 2; 34 3, 5, 3; Gradenwitz, Z SS., *Interpolationen,* 7, 76 (Romanistische Abteilung).

[1] Sherman, *Roman Law in the Modern World,* I, p. 126.

[2] Nov. c. 134, 4.

[3] C. 1, 3, 53.

clementia. Men like St. Augustine influenced not only their time but even later legislation by their juridical sagacity.

Gratian records one of St. Augustine's dicta as follows:

> "Nos in quemquam sententiam ferre non possumus, nisi aut convictum aut sponte confessum." [4]

A gloss on this particular text mentions four means of convicting an accused, *i. e.*, by law, by evident facts, by an interpretation of the law, by violent suspicion. The last the Glossator terms a presumption. The word suspicion along with its significant effect of a presumption is again employed by Pope Leo I to a Bishop Leo of Ravenna.[5] In fact Canons 110, 111, 112, and 113 of the same distinction all indicate a method of presuming baptism. Only the last chapter 113 uses the word presumption. St. Jerome in his commentary on Matthew XIX, 9, again uses the word suspicion in reference to adultery much the same as it is recorded in the Code 9, 9, 30 and the Novelles 117, c. 15. A gloss to this fragment in Gratian divides the suspicion into three classes, "probabilis, temeraria, et violenta." [6] Pope Pius I (142-157) invented the clause frequently referred to by commentators "Quia omnis suspicio potius est repellenda quam approbanda vel recipienda." [7] A commentator to the gloss here makes the simple note "Præsumptio est triplex." Gratian himself in a note to the canon calls the suspicion a "domestica præsumptio."

The application of suspicion occurs, also, in Causa II, question 1, canon 13. It is a chapter of Pseudo-Isidor.[8] The author is reputed to be Pope Melchiades (Anno 311-314) who offered the suggestion in a letter to the Bishops of Spain not to sentence anyone on the strength of a suspicion. The Canon immediately preceding bears

[4] C. 1 C. II, q. 1.

[5] 112, D. IV *De Consecratione.* Leo I (440-461 A. D.) Epistola 42, c. 1. Mansi, V, p. 1329.

[6] *Decretum Gratiani, Emendatum et Notationibus Illustratum, Una cum Glossis,* Greg. XIII, Pont. Max. iussu editum (Romae, 1582), c. 2, C. XXXII, q. 1.

[7] In his Epistle I, (M P L.), in Gratian's decree c. 9, C. VI, q. 1; Menochius, I, 7, 41-51; Reiffenstuel, *Ius Can. Univ.* II, XXIII, 2, 31; Schmalzgrueber, *Ius Eccl.,* III, XXIII, 1, 6.

[8] Hinschius, *Decretales Pseudo-Isidorianae,* (Lipsiae, 1863), p. 243, c. 2.

the title "Incerta et dubia iudicari non possunt." The Canon is an excerpt of Letter 78 #4 St. Augustine. He refers to a Canon of the III Council of Carthage.[9] Canon 15 of the same Question I reads "Manifesta accusatione non indigent," a quotation reputed to St. Ambrose (397) [10] classifying manifest acts with facta notoria.[11] St. John Chrysostom (Anno 407) in a homily on [12] Matthew V gives general rules for the indicia of time, place, will, qualities, and anything connected with the crime (homicidium) and Gratian allows the canon to end "Non enim possumus aliter ad veritatem pervenire." [13] Again, St. Augustine makes known to the one judging, that the indicia deserve consideration before sentence is passed. Here the sense [14] infers that the circumstances may indicate full proof. In c. 26, D. LXXXI, Gregory I writes that clerics are to avoid suspicion in talking to women. The Glossator adds his note that a presumption would be drawn by reason of the number (*solus ad solam*), the place, and the persons.

The indication of the burden of proof is mentioned in the Council of Sardis.[15]

The law of the Code of Justinian in reference to a negative fact, inserted in its entirety after this Canon, as well as the general principle in the following question, Canon 1,[16] indicate that the same value and force of proof is required by Gratian as exhibited in the Code, namely, "proofs brighter than the noon-day sun."[17]

[9] Cf. Harduinus—I, p. 961, Capit. VII, an. 397; c. 12, C. II, q. 1; cf. also c. 22, C. II, q. 7; c. 13, C. II, q. 7; also c. 74, C. XI, q. 3: "Grave satis est et indecens ut in re dubia certa detur sententia."

[10] Ex Commentario Ep. I ad Corinthios, M P L, Vol. 17, C. 5.

[11] D. 29, 2, 30, § 6.

[12] Matt. 5, v. 25. MPG, Vol. 49, Hom. #17; Chrysosthemos #3, p. 175-176.

[13] C. 14, C. XXIII, q. 8.

[14] *De Poenitentiae Medicina:* Sermo 35. #10; c. 75, C. XI, q. 3.

[15] Conc. Sardiscense, anno 343, c. 4, Harduinus, Conciliorum, Collectio—II, p. 640.

[16] C. 7, C. VI, q. 4 and c. 1, C. VI, q. 5; Code 4, 19, 23.

[17] C. 4, 19, 25. Cf. Hinschius, *Decretales Pseudo-Isidorianae*, p. 141, c. 17; Theod. Code liber IX, Tit. 1, c. 15; c. 2, C. II, q. 8.

Art. IV

PRESUMPTIONS IN THE COMPILATIONS AND DECRETALS

The I and II Compilations each contain titles on Presumptions that follow on the titles containing the sources for proofs. It is not strange that they were taken up later into the Decretals.

That there is reason to judge and act on human presumptions is maintained by Gregory I.

Here again it is difficult to ascertain in just what form a presumption of law exists. To a large extent it is necessary to depend on the Glossators and Commentators to determine what is in each case simply a human presumption or one of fact, or a legal presumption. Either St. Bede or St. Jerome, in commenting[1] on the Proverbs XX, 21 offers demonstration of a conjecture of fact from the present to the future.[2] Gregory I, in a letter to Bishop Victor sets up the rule of a presumption of fact that the quarrels mentioned must be public affairs in a village if the news had come to the notice of His Holiness. The Pope was employing an old presumption that information travels fast in a small locality and must be common knowledge if, also, known elsewhere.[3]

Two canons of the Council of Meaux demand the Purgatio Canonica for nuns and ecclesiastics who are suspected violently of sins of the flesh.[4] However, when a fact is not likely to happen by reason of character or reputation, or on account of suspected witnesses Alexander III presumes for the non-existence of a crime. Fama, reputation, was, then, the basis for the presumption from verisimilitude.[5]

[1] Cf. Corpus Iuris Canonici, Friedberg-Richter Editio Lipsiensis, Pars. II, *Decretalium Collectiones Lipsiae* (1922) (note 1) ad c. III, X, *De Praesumptionibus* Lib. II, Tit. XXIII, p. 353.

[2] Comp. I, c. 4, *De Praesumptionibus,* 2, 16; c. 9, X, *De Praesumptionibus,* II, 23.

[3] Comp. I, c. 9, *De Praesumptionibus,* 2, 16; c. 8, X, *De Praesumptionibus,* II 23; *Regula Iuris* #47 in VI°.

[4] Conc. Meaux (anno 845), c. 68 & c. 70, Mansi, XIV, p. 835-836; cf. Hefele, 4, 118; Comp. I, cc. 2 & 3, *De Purgatione Canonica* (5, 29); cc. 3 & 4, X, *De Purgatione Canonica,* V, 34.

[5] Comp. I, c. 10, *De Praesumptionibus* (2, 16); c. 10, X, *De Praesumptionibus,* II, 23.

Schmalzgrueber[5a] contends that this canon is a praesumptio iuris, and infers that other authors are of the same opinion. Hinschius[6] refers to this passage simply as a significant indicium, the value of which is left to the judge.[7] Reiffenstuel on the other hand classifies this canon as a violent presumption only[8] and requires that most evident arguments to the contrary would be required to overthrow it.

Alexander III enforces a praesumptio iuris in the case of espousal among persons who are physically immature.[9] In the case mentioned both parties were betrothed and lived jointly before puberty, but after becoming physically capable the woman requested a separation to marry another on the plea of non-consummation and the impediment of age. The man claimed that the marriage had been consummated. The presumption was in favor of the man as also in C. 3, C. XXXIII. q. 1, and the reason given for the faith in the man's testimony was that the husband is the superior of the wife. The law at the time required no more than that the betrothed be seven years of age.[10] This law was in reality no different than a later canon given by Gregory IX (1227-1234) in effect that a betrothal ripened into a marriage at the first act of copulation thereafter. All authors agree that this was a Praesumptio Iuris et de Iure. Certainly the espousal of immature children was no different, for as soon as they arrived at puberty and exercised conjugal rights the marriage went into immediate effect. Still, the writers maintain that in the case of children it was only a presumption of law and permitted a rebuttal. The difference is hard to discern.[11]

Nevertheless, before the canon of Gregory IX was invoked the prevailing legislation was that the betrothed who separated before the

[5a] Schmalzgrueber, *Ius Eccl.,* III, XXIII, 20.

[6] Paul, Hinschius, *Das Kirchenrecht der Katholiken und Protestanten in Deutschland,* (Berlin, *I, Guttentag, Verlagsbuchhandlung,* 1897), 6[1], p. 108.

[7] Cf. Gross, 2, 19; Hinschius, *Kirchenrecht,* V, p. 486-487.

[8] Reiffenstuel, *Ius Can. Univ.,* II, XXIII, 2, 39.

[9] Comp. I, c. 8, *De Praesumptionibus,* 4, 2.

[10] C. 8, X, *De Desponsatione Impuberum,* IV, 2.

[11] Schmalzgrueber, *Ius Eccl.,* III, XXIII, 1, 9; Reiffenstuel, *Ius Can. Univ.,* XXIII, II, 32, 51, 52; Joseph Freisen, *Geschichte des Canonischen Eherechts,* (2 ed. Paderborn, 1893), pp. 326-329.

legal age of puberty (for males 14, for females 12) were presumed by law not to be married.[12]

In the Compilatio II Clement III acting on the former judgment of Alexander III presumes the impediment of public honesty on the strength of rumor, notoriety, and on the separate oaths of the parties.[13] In the title on Presumptions Alexander III conjectures from proximate circumstances the act itself.[14] It is the famous case cited by all authors to indicate a violent presumption. Not only is the example striking, but the jurisprudence of Alexander III is to be considered, for here he definitely passes sentence in a criminal matter on the strength of a violent presumption of man.

In the matter of proof the presumption of consummation is overcome by Gregory VIII on the testimony of seven women and the oath of the party to prove virginity even against the oath of the man who swore to the contrary.[15] Schmalzgrueber and Reiffenstuel both claim[16] this to be a praesumptio iuris. In II Compilatio a rule is set up by Clement III in reference to marriages entered into under force and fear. Here the law read that if a person had entered marriage with undue pressure after a year and a half of cohabitation the marriage cause could not be contested in so far as it was presumed iuris et de iure that the person consented then to the marriage.[17] The canon reads on,

> . . . Nec de cetero recipiendi sunt testes, si quos memorata mulier ad probandum, quod non consenserit in eundem nomi-

[12] Comp. I, c. 14, *De Desponsatione Impuberum* (4, 2); C. 10, X, *De Desponsatione Impuberum,* IV, 2.

[13] Comp. II, c. 8, *De Sponsabilibus et Matrimonio,* (4, 1); C. 13, X, *De Praesumptionibus,* II, 23; Menochius, *De Praesumptionibus,* I, 94, 3 & 4; Reiffenstuel, *Ius Can. Univ.*, II, XXIII, 2, 34.

[14] Comp. II, c. 2, *De Praesumptionibus,* 2, 15; c. 12, X, *De Praesumptionibus,* II, 23.

[15] Comp. II, c. 2, *De Probationibus,* 2, 10; c. 4, X, *De Probationibus,* II, 19.

[16] Schmalzgrueber, *Ius Eccl.,* III, XXIII, 1, 10; Reiffenstuel, *Ius Can. Univ.,* II, XXIII, 2, 51.

[17] Comp. II, c. 7, *De Sponsalibus et Matrimonio,* 4, 1; c. 21, X, *De Sponsalibus et Matrimonio,* IV, 1; Schmalzgrueber, *Ius Eccl.,* IV, 1, 401; Reiffenstuel, *Ius Can. Univ.* II, XXIII, II, 52. Freisen, *Kanonische Eherecht,* p. 276, n. 53; p. 270-275.

naverit producendos, quum mora tanti temporis huiusmodi probationem excludat. . . .

From the references advanced it will be noted that it is extremely difficult not only to discover a genuine presumption of law, but even to establish the rules for saying precisely where a typical *praesumptio iuris* is introduced in the law. Of the sixteen canons mentioned in the chapter on Presumptions in the Decretals only one, canon 11, might be classified as such.[18] In other titles throughout the Decretals presumptions of law are more evident; at least at that particular era they could be classified according to the jurisprudence in practice. The closing lines of Canon 3 of Book III, Title 43 of the Decretals might well be called an established praesumptio iuris.

> . . . Et certe de illo, qui natus de Christianis parentibus, et inter Christianos est fideliter conversatus, tam violenter praesumitur, quod fuerit baptizatus, ut haec praesumptio pro certitudine sit habenda, donec evidentissimis forsitan argumentis contrarium probaretur.[19]

That the sentence of a judge is presumed to have been given in accordance with due process of law was introduced into the legislation by Clement III in 1202.[20] A presumption against a judge's ability would require exacting proof. Clement calls such a presumption frivolous. However, to safeguard official actions from such attacks a law was drafted in the Fourth Lateran Council a short time later requiring a public authority (or two competent men) to act as notary during an entire process. The presumption introduced into the law put full faith in the notary's transcriptions and documents, but limited the judge to these alone as his sources for passing sentence. On the other hand the presumption would fall in case he neglected to record the proceedings.[21]

[18] C. II, X, *De Praesumptionibus*, II, 23.

[19] Cf. Comp. III, C. Un., *De Presbytero non Baptizato*, 5, 22.

[20] Glossa ad c. 6, X, *De Renunciatione*, I, 9: ". . . Item semper praesumitur pro sententia donec in contrarium ostendatur. . . ."

[21] Conc. Lateran IV, c. 38; Mansi, XXII, p. 1023; C. 11, X, *De Probationibus*, II, 19.

The one case mentioned by all commentators as a genuine presumptio iuris et de iure is contained in the Decretals of Gregory IX.[22] The case is as follows: a betrothal was made between a man and woman to marry in the future and before this marriage took place they had sexual intercourse with each other. In this event the law presumed marriage had taken place and with such effect that no proof to the contrary was admitted. The canon reads further that even should the man marry another and consummate this second union it would be invalid. A gloss to this canon reads

> "Nota circa huiusmodi praesumptiones quae praesumptio alia est iuris et canonis sive legis, alia hominis alia naturae, alia facti. Praesumptio iuris et canonis, sive legis, sive de iure quod idem est non recipit probationem in contrarium."

It might well be inferred that the strength of the praesumptio iuris et de iure during the time of the Glossators lay in the reason that no proofs were permitted to the contrary. To this observation Hinschius remarks that the praesumptio iuris et de iure is equivalent to a fictio iuris in as much as the truth is prescribed in spite of the fact that the very opposite may be true. He concludes that the only difference between the two is that the fictio is set up even when the truth is known.[23] This was unquestionably the prevailing opinion for Menochius records the concepts of the iuris et de iure praesumptio among commentators in much the same style.[24] In his Speculum Iuris under Praesumptio Iuris et de Iure Speculator, Guilelmus Durantis (1237-1296) calls a necessary presumption a praesumptio iuris et de iure.[25]

[22] C. 30, X, *De Sponsalibus et Matrimoniis,* IV, 1; Zallinger, *Institutiones Iuris Eccelesiastici* (Romae, 1923), Liber II, Decretalium, p. 208; Schmalzgrueber, *Ius Eccl.,* III, XXIII, 1, 9; Reiffenstuel, *Ius Can. Univ.,* II, XXIII, 26 and 52; Hinschius, *Kirchenrecht,* 6^1, p. 105, n. 4; Menochius, *De Praesumptionibus,* I, 76, 1.

[23] Hinschius, *Kirchenrecht,* 6^1, p. 105, n. 3.

[24] Menochius, *De Praesumptionibus,* I, 3.

[25] Durantis, *Speculum Iuris,* II, 2, De Praesump. § Species, #5: "Necessaria autem est praesumptio illa, quam communiter vocant Magistri, iuris et de iure, et haec inducit probationem, et iudicem ad pronunciandum nec recipit probationem in contrarium. . . ." Also, Menochius, *De Praesumptionibus,* I, 3, 9.

Menochius continues that this violent presumption becomes more effective if drawn from the course of natural events:

> ". . . Cum haec aliter se habere possit, quam reipso sit: attamen vix fieri potest, quod contrariam probationem admittat."

In support of this view he mentions Baldus in his commentary on Digest 47, 2, 3. In #13 of the same question Menochius [26] expresses the general view of several commentators in the words:

> "Lex enim ita praesumit ut verum illud esse statuat, contrariumque probari non posse decernat. Nam legis auctoritas hoc certum esse facit."

That this was not only private opinion or law-school teaching, but the law itself may be gathered from the Statutum Venetum #10 of the second prologue wherein is stated that a contrary proof to a praesumptio iuris et de iure was not admitted. There was apparently a sanction added to the effect presumed by the law to prevent any attempt to demonstrate the contrary. It should also be noted that these writers carried their notion of praesumptio iuris et de iure into Canon Law and offered their opinions on the texts under consideration to Canon 30, X, *De Sponsalibus et Matrimoniis,* IV, 1, and canons 8 and 10, X, *De Praesumptionibus,* II, 23. Freisen claims that during this age (Thirteenth Century) there was a strong inclination to presume anything and the reason seems to have been to prevent the dissolution of marriages on statements of the parties.[27] Wherein the essence of marriage consisted was disputed whether in the sponsalia de praesenti or de futuro, with or without a subsequent copula carnalis or with or without affectus maritalis.[28] The praesumptio iuris et de iure is not so evident in the decree "Per tuas" [29] whereas, it is most apparent in "Is qui fidem." [30]

[26] Menochius, *De Praesumptionibus,* I, 3, 9; Baldus, Grammaticus, Alciatus, Curtius Iunior, Felimus, Romanus.

[27] Freisen, *Kanonische Eherecht,* p. 210, n. 71.

[28] Freisen, *Kanonische Eherecht,* p. 205.

[29] C. 6, X, *De Conditionibus,* IV, 5.

[30] C. 30, X, *De Desponsalibus,* IV, 2.

The Council of Trent by means of the celebrated *Tametsi* attempted to abolish this *praesumptio iuris et de iure* by making marriage not contracted before the pastor and two witnesses invalid.[31] Marriages contracted contrary to this form were known thereafter as clandestine. But the *Tametsi* was enforced only in those territories in which it was promulgated or in use by custom. Another act of legislation was enacted to avoid the abuses of clandestine marriage. The abuse the Holy Father referred to was the interpretation given the concept of *affectus maritalis.* In effect the *copula cum affectu maritali* was equivalent to consent and actually produced a marriage between those engaged or those who contracted with a pending condition in the same manner that consent effects marriage in *Canon Law* today. If copulation was performed without the *affectus maritalis* the act was sinful and fornicarious, but did not bring a marriage into existence, at least in the internal forum.

Consequently, Leo XIII in the decree "*Consensus Mutuus*" enacted that henceforth the old Decretals were abolished and that a *copula* subsequent to betrothal would not effect a valid marriage in either forum.[32]

Reiffenstuel also records the canon given by Clement V in the Council of Vienne in reference to Letters of the Pope as containing irrebuttable presumptions.[33] Its value lies in the fact that once letters have been issued by the Holy Father the facts contained therein on which the Holy Father bases his right cannot be questioned.

In the Extravagantes of John XXII, in Title V the Glossator adds to the closing lines "cum non sit verisimile" etc. "iuris vel de iure" and concluded that this is equivalent to a violent presumption and that this is the same as a fiction of law.[34]

Freisen's observation in regard to the facility and frequency of

[31] Conc. Trid., sess., 24, *De Reformatione Matr.*, cap. I.

[32] Leo XIII, decr. "*Consensus Mutuus,*" 15 febr., 1892,—*Fontes* n. 613; cf., *Coll. S. C. Prop. Fid.*, II, n. 1786; *ASS*, XIII, 16-18.

[33] Reiffenstuel, *Ius Can. Univ.*, II, XXIII, 1, 26.

[34] Glossa ad Extravagantes John XXII, tit. V. "Non sit verisimile" scilicet iuris praesumptione contra quam et alias admitti possit probatio . . . ubi tamen iuris praesumptio transit in violentam ut quia est iuris vel de iure, non est ita, quia tunc magis dicitur fictio.

presuming during the age of Gregory and the Glossators is most pertinent.

The ability to draw a presumption was most sinned against by the Glossators and commentators. If the authors of the fifteenth and sixteenth centuries that immediately followed them are any reflection of their teachers there is ample demonstration of their art in their writings. Menochius' copious work of six books comprising almost 700 questions on all possible subjects and his numerous references is sufficient evidence. Besides, he is only one of the scholars of his time who attempted such a task. To Alciatus is attributed a similar accomplishment.

The astounding part of all their constant presuming is that no precise rules were determined to fix presumptions definitely by law. If any underlying inference were discovered either in Civil or Canon Law it was invoked immediately, said to be implicitly contained in a law or canon, and applied in all similar cases.[35] In other words each author took it upon himself to read into a law a *praesumptio iuris* or even *iuris et de iure,* as he perceived the jurisprudence to be exercised in each case. Reiffenstuel gives clear terse explanations of presumptions in a methodical manner with succinct clearness, but falls into the same practice as his predecessors of misinterpreting presumptions of law with presumptions of man, based on the comments of the Glossators.[36] He reveals, too, the tendency then in force to classify the value of testimony into *probationes plenae* and *semi-plenae.* Thus in Par. II, #32 he very well states that the general practice is to leave this matter entirely to the prudence of the judge who by way of induction is to decide whether a conclusion from indications is a mere suspicion, a probable, or a violent presumption.

In section 34 following he indicates that a probable presumption of man would be only half proof, while at the close of section

[35] Menochius, *De Praesumptionibus,* I, 5, 19: ". . . Crediderim tamen quod etsi praesumptio et coniectura aliqua scripta non est in lege, si tamen magnam cum scripta affinitatem habet & similitudinem, quod contingit ob maiorem, vel eandem rationem, de ea iudicandum erit quo ad sui effectum, quod de ipsa scripta. Cum enim casus omnes lege comprehendi minime potuerint, de similibus ad similia procedimus. . . . ."

[36] Reiffenstuel, *Ius. Can. Univ.,* II, XXIII, I, 19 and 20.

35 he states that two such half proofs would constitute one full proof. The apparent difficulty was the confounding of the two forms of presumption of law and of fact, and also the more general custom of interpreting the *indicia* as *presumptiones*.[37] Contrary to the present legislation Reiffenstuel also asserts that the burden of proof could be shifted by the judge on a presumption of fact. In the example he proposes from Bartolus about determining majority in minors he evidently misconstrues the nature of the issue and the general teaching on the burden of proof. The principle in both Roman and Canon law was simple, "Ei incumbit probatio qui dicit, non qui negat." [38] The application was contained in another fragment, "Semper necessitas probandi incumbit illi, qui agit." [39] Still another qualifying law was necessary in justice, hence, ". . . in exceptionibus dicendum est, reum partibus actoris fungi opportere."[40] In the case adduced by Reiffenstuel the actor is asserting a negative fact, namely, that X is under 25 years, that he is a minor. To deny such a statement is the right of the defendant forcing the plaintiff to the burden of proof. Should the actor contend that X has asserted he is a major and must prove it, is a complete misunderstanding of procedure. Whoever founds his contention on a negative fact has the burden of proof. Furthermore, the *reus* in taking exception becomes the *actor* and is forced to prove his allegations, also, whether in the exception he asserts or denies.[41] This is exactly one of the striking differences between a presumption of law and of man; that of law shifts the burden of proof where that of man does not. If the latter did, the plaintiff could set up any number of light presumptions and so force the defendant to the proof instead of undertaking the burden himself. "Qui probare tenetur, non nudis coniecturis incedere debet." [42] In the interpretation of the *factum negativum* Reiffenstuel was probably influenced by the Glossa to

[37] Hinschius, *Kirchenrecht,* 6, 1, pp. 107 & 108, note 1.

[38] D. 22, 3, 2.

[39] D. 22, 3, 21.

[40] D. 22, 3, 19; 3, 25, § 2.

[41] Winscheid-Kipp, *Lehrbuch Des Pandektenrechts,* I, p. 675, note 4.

[42] F. Lucii Ferraris, *Bibliotheca,* Tomus 6, (ed., Romae 1890), Ex Typographia Polyglotta S.C. De Prop. Fide., p. 384, "Praesumptio" #10. Additiones ex aliena manu. Roberti, *De Processibus,* II, pp. 27, 28 & 29.

c. 23, X, *De Electione,* I, 6, where the principle from the Code of Justinian is quoted with a slight variation C. 4, 19, 23: ". . . cum per rerum naturam factum negantis nulla probatio sit." The same principle is quoted again in c. 11, X, *De Probationibus,* II, 19, and referred to in Canon 12 of the same title. The general interpretation prevailed that "facta negativa" that were purely negative without any relation to time and place could not be proved.[43]

The manner in which Schmalzgrueber follows in the footsteps of Reiffenstuel of the commentators is apparent. Apart from the diversity of quotations the doctrine is the same. Where the rule in reference to the *praesumptio iuris et de iure* had been to exclude all proof to the contrary, Schmalzgrueber (more prolix than Reiffenstuel) demonstrates the exceptions to this rule as follows:

1) By indirect proof, demonstrating that the foundation on which the presumption rests does not exist.[44] This same rule is in effect to-day.

2) By demonstrating the truth; if the doubt, the pivotal point of a presumption is removed, the presumption falls. The truth may be a notorious fact, but, he contends, it must be introduced during the process.[45]

3) By an extra-judicial confession by the person in whose favor the presumption stands since a confession is always regarded as the best proof of the truth.[46]

4) Testimony of witnesses to the contrary. It was uncertain at the time of Schmalzgrueber how many witnesses were necessary to overthrow a presumptio iuris et de iure.[47]

5) By a public document which is equal to confession and always carries with it the presumption of full truth.

[43] Cf. Schmalzgrueber, *Ius. Eccl.,* III, XIX, 11, 38; Wernz-Vidal, *Ius Canonicum* (Romae, 1927), VI, p. 378; Zallinger, *Decretalium,* II, XIX, 230.

[44] Schmalzgrueber, *Ius Eccl.,* III, XXIII, 12. Cf. Menochius, *De Praesumptionibus* I, 65, 1.

[45] Menochius, *De Praesumptionibus,* I, 67, 1; Schmalzgrueber, *Ius Eccl.,* III, XXIII, 12.

[46] Menochius, *De Praesumptionibus,* I, 61, 1 & 16; Schmalzgrueber, *Ius Eccl.,* III, XXIII, 1, 13.

[47] Menochius believes that two or three well qualified witnesses would suffice while Schmalzgrueber records that some authors require five.

6) By proof submitted without objection from the party in possession of the presumption in which event the person was believed to have renounced his right.

There is little or no difference today in the method of proof against a presumptio iuris et de iure. The presentation of Schmalzgrueber is very much the same in Wernz-Vidal, but it is called indirect proof,[48] since the presumption itself is not attacked, but only its foundation. Should one hold fast to the law as enunciated in the Decretals[49] one would be employing a fiction of law once the truth were known. To maintain the concept of presumption it is mandatory to permit proof to the contrary.[50] From the time of the Decretals there was no active and general change in the legislation. Some general and private instructions were given in which the use of presumptions was outlined and directed. Thus, in the Instruction of the Holy Office of November 17, 1830, three rules were laid down in cases of doubtful baptism (whether a *dubium iuris* or *dubium facti*). When no moral certainty was attainable by direct testimony recourse is to be made to indirect proof, or presumptions.[51] Later on August 1, 1883, Bishop Gross of Savannah received a reply on the rules to be applied in his diocese in establishing the fact of baptism when in doubt.[52] This same instruction was adopted in the III Plenary Council of Baltimore in its entirety.[53] Another instruction was issued previously on May 13, 1868, by the Holy Office on the method of establishing the fact of death of one spouse. This instruction [54] was also introduced in the Third Plenary Council of Baltimore and reproduced in the Acta Apostolicae Sedis in 1910.[55] In the instruction of the Sacred Congregation of Bishops and Regulars of June 11, 1880, in reference to Criminal Procedure for clerics Article 16 repeats the principle that had been con-

[48] Wernz-Vidal, *Ius Canonicum,* VI, p. 468, note 16.

[49] C. 30, X, *De Sponsalibus et Matrimoniis,* IV, 1.

[50] Wernz-Vidal, l.c.

[51] *Fontes,* n. 869.

[52] *Fontes,* n. 1083.

[53] *Conc. Plen. Balt. III,* appendix p. 246.

[54] *Conc. Plen. Balt. III,* p. 258.

[55] *A.A.S.,* II, (1910), 199—. Ayrinhac—Lydon: *Marriage Legislation in the New Code of Canon Law* (Benziger Bros. 1934), pp. 132-135.

stantly in vogue.[56] While neither article 15 nor 16 contains any word about presumptions it is quite apparent that in many such delicts of criminal nature no proof could be obtained unless the use of ordinary presumptions were permitted. Ordinary presumptions of man could very well lead to moral certainty.

In retrospect it can be said that the general practice of setting up presumptions has been in force in Church Law since its inception based on the practice in use in Roman Law. The rules and method of determining the classification and value were undetermined. It remained alone for the Code of Canon Law to clarify this moot question by relieving the judge from determining a presumption of law and the rule of procedure in shifting the burden of proof. Consequently, on Pentecost, May 19, 1918, by the act of promulgation Rome settled a matter that had been battered from pillar to post by jurists for years and set up for procedure the four canons enumerated in the Fourth Book of the Code in Canons 1825-1828. Hence, today it is certain that only those Canons contain Praesumptiones Iuris in which they are expressed by law; all other presumptions are of man.[57] Further, it is not within the competence of any author (iudex) to read legal presumptions into the law; canon 1828 very definitely divides presumptions into two classes as well as canon 1825. "Praesumptiones quae non statuuntur a iure" signifies the only other alternative: "praesumptio hominis."

[56] *Fontes,* n. 2005. Cf. Droste-Messmer, *Canonical Procedure in Disciplinary and Criminal Cases of Clerics,* Benziger Bros. (New York, 1887), p. 125.

[57] Canon 1825.

PART II

PRESUMPTIONS OF LAW IN MARRIAGE CASES

CHAPTER I

Canon 1014

ART. I. FAVOR IURIS

Can. 1014.—"Matrimonium gaudet favore iuris; quare in dubio standum est pro valore matrimonii, donec contrarium probetur, salvo praescripto Can. 1127."

"Marriage enjoys the favor of the law; therefore, when in doubt the validity of marriage must be upheld until the contrary is demonstrated, save for the regulation of Canon 1127."

This Canon may well be termed the pivotal point of all matrimonial procedure, for no matter on what score a marriage is attacked, the plaintiff will be immediately confronted with this law. In its *wording* and *operation* it is a typical *praesumptio iuris,* i.e., the plaintiff is forced to prove either that this so-called matrimonial contract now questioned has not the semblance of marriage and never took place, or, that because of some invalidating reason it was null *ab initio.*[1]

That facts should not be presumed is only reasonable; they must be proved. Even when called in doubt if there are no witnesses to the fact, it is sufficient to have circumstances that indicate an event, especially to preserve the validity of subsequent acts contingent upon the fact.[2]

In reality, then, some facts are presumed, but so determined by norms derived from cases in which such facts frequently occur, that the facts are said to be proved.[3] It is supposed that a logical deduction

[1] Cf. Chelodi, *Ius Matrimoniale,* (3 ed. Tridenti, 1921), p. 6.

[2] Menochius, *De Praesumptionibus,* 6, 4, 1 and 2; Maroto, *Institutiones,* I, p. 224.

[3] C. 3, X, *De Presbytero non Baptizato,* III, 43; Menochius, *De Praesumptionibus,* III, 1, 1; IX, 14, 1.

is made from the circumstances and not one irrelevant to the indications. While this Canon takes in both the doubt of fact as well as the question of validity the latter is the one which arises more frequently. Facts are more easily established even by the indirect means of presumptions. Marriages are more readily attacked for invalidity. Since the law is dealing with human affairs in which there is always liable to be error or fraud the marriage is immediately taken into possession by the law and strongly guarded.

Doubts may be injected with almost any of the impediments to marriage, either one or many, as ligamen, sacred orders, consanguinity, crime; the true and free consent may be brought into question by alleging simulation, force, fear, or error; or the requisite antecedents, of which the most important is baptism and the freedom to marry, proper dispensations, perhaps interpellations, and formalities, competence, or the correct form, may be deficient or of such an incorrect nature as to make one reasonably doubt the validity of a marriage. It is when such doubts can not be resolved that the law of Canon 1014 goes into effect and renders its statement that there is not sufficient reason to declare the marriage questioned invalid.[4]

The value of Canon 1014 becomes most obvious in the face of discovering an antecedent marriage or when attempts are made at subsequent marriages. The Canon embraces all possible situations. If a marriage were contracted *in facie Ecclesiae* and both parties, of which one or both were previously married, deceived the priest as to their free state there is no question about the internal forum. According to moral theology they are living not in concubinage, but in adultery. If one party was in good faith it is not correct upon the first notice to decide against the marriage. The favor of the law insists that this union is valid until it is definitely proved that a first existed. The situation may easily arise, although frequently fraud is intended to obviate the restrictions of the Church. Error in such matters may also be present, especially in countries of mixed religion.

A hypothetical case of *dubium facti*. Young people seeking em-

[4] The Rota decisions of validity on marriage are proposed as a *dubium*, e.g. "An constet de matrimonii nullitate in casu." The response refers to the doubt with either "constare" or "non constare."

ployment journey in large numbers to a metropolis. To seek advantage and cheaper living a young man A, and woman B, enter into a genuine common law marriage without a public record and without witnesses. A is a baptized Protestant, B, a baptized Catholic, born of a mixed marriage and raised in infidelity. They know that a common law marriage is recognized civilly in the jurisdiction in which they are living. They cohabit for a year and the marriage is without issue. Because of lack of employment the girl, B, leaves for her home. When taking convert instructions she discovers the necessity of form in marriage for Catholics and is convinced that since she is baptized and because of lack of proper form she had not contracted a valid marriage with A. She presents herself with another man C, a Catholic, to the pastor for marriage and insists that she had never been married before. She is also mindful that A can not prove the previous marriage by a document or witnesses to the contract. A second marriage is contracted in due form with a Catholic. The first man returns to contest the marriage. The girl admits concubinage, but no marriage. The procedure of the Church would be to maintain the second union, contracted *in facie Ecclesiae* as valid and grant it all the protection of the law until ligamen of the first marriage could be demonstrated. Since B, although baptized, was not bound by the form, and since there were no witnesses to the contract a series of indications and circumstances would be required to overthrow the presumption of the law. Witnesses, two well qualified, could testify that A and B were regarded as man and wife, they referred to one another as such; A has receipt from jeweler for the ring, B wore the ring constantly, they contracted obligations jointly as married people, as, bank account, charge account, installment plan purchases; the landlord believed they were married; no one ever heard B deny she was A's wife. All these indications including the admitted concubinage by B would build up a violent presumption that ligamen existed and upset the presumption of 1014. Public opinion in the United States is opposed to open concubinage so that the presumption would favor some type of marriage from testimonies and indications.

Case of doubtful validity. A, a widower, is president of a large bank that had several runs on it before the bank holiday. He had been friendly with a wealthy woman B, of advanced age and because of the bad situation of his bank was anxious to stem the tide of public opinion against his financial institution. During the critical period the newspapers carried at great length details of a quiet, but socially important wedding between A and B. The wedding was celebrated *in facie Ecclesiae* and was in every external detail valid. The event saved the financial situation and the two people lived under the same roof for three months. The strain of the financial crisis and the concomitant reaction injured A's health so that he became seriously ill. In spite of the cohabitation and on account of the illness, A contended in civil court that the marriage was never consummated. A decree of civil annulment was granted for non fulfillment of contract. After due process of investigation A's plea for a dispensation *super rato et non-consummato* was refused. He now alleges fictitious consent as the real cause on which to base his annulment. The primary cause of lack of consent was the precarious financial condition of the bank. The press notices describing the consolidation of wealth saved the situation. He maintained cohabitation without consummation, but during the illness only, to insure the safety of the bank. B was unaware of the ruse, and was no party to such an agreement. A's business associates admit the runs on the bank, but deny the institution was insolvent, and had no knowledge that A even contemplated such a step to insure their finances.

Preceding the marriage A was wont to be in the company of various women, but with B particularly on fashionable and expensive occasions. There were no differences or quarrels after the marriage. B still professes deep affection for A and wishes to do all for his happiness.

In the face of such little external evidence in spite of the alleged good cause the marriage would still be in possession and be presumed valid. The presumptions and evidence to outweigh the force of Canon 1014 would necessarily have to be more convincing.

In a petition sent to Rome by the Vicars Apostolic of Central Oceanica in 1872 the question was raised if the opposite principle, *"in dubio standum esse pro invaliditate matrimonii,"* might not be put into practice due to the difficulty experienced by the missionaries in attempting to establish the fact of marriage among pagans. The decision of the Holy Office given in the instruction was that although it may seem equitable to depart from the original principle in cases of doubt as to the real existence of a marriage, nevertheless, when a marriage can show possession for itself the contrary rule to maintain invalidity must not be applied.[5]

There is a definite application of Canon 1014 in the Code itself in Canon 1070 §2. While, before the promulgation of the Code, a doubtful baptism was always presumed valid, even among non-Catholics, *in ordine ad matrimonium,* Canon 1070 §2, insists that the validity of the marriage is to be maintained no matter how strong the presumption may be for invalid baptism until it is *certain* that one party is a baptized Catholic and the other is not baptized. Should the doubt of baptism be unsolvable, the presumptions of baptism do not come into play, but a new principle that the marriage must be maintained as valid.[5a]

The Code makes an exception in Canon 1127 in matters of doubt in favor of the faith. The inverse presumption would be in place here, namely, "In matters of doubt to favor the True Faith the law favors invalidity." The ultimate reason for applying Canon 1127 is not so much that the doubt can not be solved, but that the Canon comprises cases where the conditions for the use of the *Pauline Privilege* are doubtful. While this is a wide concession on the part of the legislator the Canon has limitations.

The *Privilegium Fidei* differs from the *Privilegium Paulinum* by its wider comprehension. In the Pauline Privilege the starting point is always a marriage between two pagans, two persons certainly not baptized, living in a valid union called *matrimonium legitimum.* In the *privilegium fidei* the union is also *legitimum,* not *ratum,* between a baptized person and a pagan, or, also, two pagans. Since such a marriage is not ratum, even if consummated, it is within the

[5] S.C.S. Officii, Instr., (ad Vicarios Apostolicos Oceaniae Centralis), Dec. 18, 1872,—*Fontes* n. 1024; Gasparri, *De Matrimonio* (1932), I, 25.

[5a] In reference to doubtful baptism of Canon 1070 see Schenk, *Mixed Religion and Disparity of Cult,* (Washington, D. C., 1929), pp. 119-146.

plenitude of the Sovereign Pontiff to dissolve such a marriage, when a doubt cannot be resolved, in favor of the faith.[6] The law of Canon 1127 would embrace for the purposes of the following consideration these cases:

1) Marriage between two pagans doubtful either of fact or of validity and if one party becomes a Catholic;

2) Marriage between a doubtfully baptized Protestant and a pagan: a) if pagan becomes a Christian and marriage is not consummated; b) if Protestant becomes a Catholic, even if marriage is later consummated, but the pagan gives reason for separation.

In the case of two doubtfully baptized Protestants authors are at variance. The preferred opinion seems to be that their marriage can not be dissolved since there would be a danger of dissolving a *ratum et consummatum* union.[7]

The Code also definitely forbids a marriage to be dissolved where a Catholic enters a union with an infidel or a doubtfully baptized person with a dispensation of *disparity of worship*.[8] Triebs' reference that the presumption employed in Canon 1127 is a *praesumptio iuris et de iure* can hardly be correct.[9] In the application of the Canon 1127 the presumption of a valid marriage yields to a privilege of the True Faith. If the conditions for the use of the Pauline Privilege are doubtful and the privilege in favor of the True Faith is applied, a marriage that under Canon 1014 would be presumed valid is dissolved. However, should it be discovered later after a second marriage has been contracted that one or both parties successfully concealed facts and obtained freedom of the bond by fraud, the existence of the first marriage would necessarily have to be upheld.

[6] Gasparri, *De Matrimonio* II, 204; 233-234; Wernz-Vidal, *Ius Canonicum,* V, 774. Cf. Paul III, Const., *"Altitudo,"* 7 June, 1537; St. Pius, V, Const., *"Romani Pontificis,"* 2 August, 1571; Gregory XIII, Const., *"Populis,"* 25 January, 1585. These constitutions are in the appendix of the Code, Documents VI, VII, VIII respectively.

[7] Cf. Vermeersch-Creusen, *Epitome,* II, p. 251; Triebs, *Handbuch des Kanon. Eherechts,* IV, 725; Ayrinhac-Lydon, *Marriage Legislation,* p. 327; Gregory, *The Pauline Privilege* (Washington, D. C., 1931), pp. 124-129.

[8] Gasparri, *De Matrimonio,* p. 240; Canon 1120, § 2; Triebs, *Handbuch des Kanonischen Eherechts,* IV, p. 725.

[9] Triebs, *Handbuch des Kanonischen Eherechts,* IV, 725.

Furthermore, to contend that Canon 1127 is a *praesumptio iuris et de iure* would mean that when this type of marriage case is judged it becomes a *res iudicata*—which is not true of marriage cases except as to civil effects. Hence, if, in the solution of the doubt, Canon 1127 is used and if a presumption is therein contained it can be no more than a praesumptio iuris.

Any union that can claim the *species matrimonii* for itself is an established fact. The only manner in which it could be questioned is in regard to its validity. Therefore, marriage is in possession of the law, is protected thereby, and enjoys all the effects of the connubial state of life; e. g., the children are legitimate, the union is indissoluble, there are mutual rights and obligations, etc.

Reiffenstuel on two occasions mentions in no uncertain words the value of *praesumptio iuris* in this regard. At one time he asserts, "Praesumptio illa, quae facit, valere actum, est regina aliarum praesumptionum,"[10] and again, "Praesumptio iuris est liquidissima probatio, nisi contraria probatione elidatur."[11]

The underlying principle of these rules is that all acts once performed are supposed valid.[12]

In regard to marriage Canon 1014 is the juridical counterpart of the Church's doctrine on the indissolubility. This is only one of the presumptions in legislation on marriage, founded either on fact or for the general welfare of society.[13]

In questions of validity the marriage bond must be given security from some source, otherwise there would be present the continual risk of voiding a sacramental contract and "putting asunder what God hath joined."[14]

[10] Reiffenstuel, *Ius Can. Univ.*, II, XXIII, 91; Menochius, *De Praesumptionibus,* I, 29, 3; VI, 2; VI, 4, 1 and 2.

[11] Reiffenstuel, *Ius Can. Univ.*, II, XXIII, 48.

[12] D. 34, 5, 12 (13); 45, 1, 80; 22, 3, 5.

[13] Cf. Canon 21.

[14] Matthew V, 32; XIX, 9; Ephesians V, 32; Gasparri, *De Matrimonio,* II, p. 24; c. 47, X, *De Testibus et Attestationibus* II, 20, "Tolerabilius est enim, aliquas contra statuta hominum dimittere copulatos, quam coniunctos legitime contra statuta Domini separare." S.R. Rotae Decisiones, IV (1912), 16 and 37.

Art. II. Mors Praesumpta

Should a marriage have been contracted and a second one be contemplated the first step is to establish the necessary freedom from the former marriage in order that the second union be a valid and licit one. In proving death of a former spouse the ordinary method is by means of documents either civil or ecclesiastical. However, if the matter of death is not established in this fashion when one party has disappeared or been absent for a long time, an investigation must be made. To attempt to contract another marriage before this is established is to run counter to the prohibition in Canon 1069 §2, and the general teaching of the Church that forbids adultery or simultaneous bigamy.

The investigation must be made by the bishop or ordinary who must institute at least a summary process if not a solemn trial to establish with moral certitude that the absent party is not among the living.[15]

According to the Instruction given by the Holy Office to establish the death of one spouse juridically[16] the proofs that are admitted are as follows: 1) a death certificate of either civil or ecclesiastical authority; this constitutes full proof, providing it originates from the territory in which the person died. However, a civil declaration of death is not conclusive proof;[17] 2) in the absence of a death certificate the deposition of two eyewitnesses above suspicion, given under oath and substantiating one another in reference to the fact and concomitant circumstances; 3) the testimony of one witness may be accepted if his deposition is trustworthy and is substantiated by sufficient adminicular proof; 4) hearsay witnesses who can testify that they heard at an unsuspecting time from others of the death of the spouse in question from eyewitnesses who are distant and who can not testify at the present moment. Their testimony must conform with that of one another and be supported by the concomitant

[15] S. C. S. Off., 27 April, 1887: "Saltem summarie et extraiudicialiter." Neque necessarius est interventus defensoris vinculi, S. C. C. 14 Dec., 1889, *ASS,* XXII, 546.

[16] S. C. S. Off., 13 maii, 1868—*Fontes* n. 1002; Conc. Plen. Balt. III, Appendix p. 258.

[17] Cf. *LQS,* 75 (1922), 683.

circumstances; 5) presumptions and conjectures that will establish moral certitude for a prudent judge are also accepted as proof.

Before advancing into the value of these presumptions to establish presumed death the *status quaestionis* must be stated, namely, the fact of the first marriage is certain and that one party has disappeared. The presumption to be overthrown is that as long as there is no moral certitude that a person is dead he is presumed to be still among the living. Besides solemn profession, a Papal dispensation *super rato,* and the use of the *Pauline Privilege* or the *Privilege of the True Faith,* the only cause, and the most natural one, of dissolution of marriage already contracted is death of one of the parties to the contract.

Another observation must not be overlooked. If a second marriage is contested because the death of one of the parties of a first marriage is not definitely and certainly known, the second marriage will be declared at least illicit if not invalid because of a previous existing fact of marriage. All that need be demonstrated is the fact of the first marriage. Whether this first marriage was invalid is another question. As long as it exists and can show the *species matrimonii* it will be in possession. The validity will then be maintained until the contrary is known. The moot question in the matter of presumed death is not the validity of the first marriage, but its existence, and as long as the death of one party is not established the other party is forbidden to enter another union due to the possibility of an invalid second marriage. A response of the Holy Office confirms this.

> "1. Titio capto a rebellibus, eoque frustra per duos aut tres annos desiderato, Martha eius uxor sine assistentia proprii sacerdotis, quae ad valorem ibi necessaria non est, et contra monitum missionariorum, contraxit cum Marco. Marcus autem graviter reprehensus a missionariis, vult quidem dimittere Martham, sed petit ad alias transire nuptias. Quid agendum?
>
> 2. Caecilia, marito a rebellibus capto, nec post tres annos amplius comparente, eum habuit pro mortuo, et, absente proprio sacerdote, nupsit Petro rei conscio, sed similiter de morte pioris viri persuaso. Missionarius cum impossibile

sit scire vel inquirere utrum Paulus vir prior vivat, censet eos non esse inquietandos, et relinquendos esse in martrimonio donec non habeatur certus nuntius de vita Pauli. An bene?

R. Ad 1. Separandos esse coniuges, et virum non posse secundas inire nuptias, usque dum moraliter sit certum, quo tempore ipse matrimonium iniit cum muliere de qua agitur, primum virum eiusdem mulieris non obiise.

Ad. 2. Relinquendos esse in bona fide."[18]

A closer examination of this response will reveal that there was present the initial presumption that Titius was dead since to have been captured by, perhaps, bandits meant certain death. There would be more reason to believe that the absence meant death than that he was still living. Hence, to avert the danger of voiding the second marriage the Holy Office with more than a reasonable doubt decided that Marcus could not contract a second union.

In the second case the conditions were more favorable, since the parties were *bona fide* and convinced of the death of the departed spouse, and had presumptions indicative of death after capture by bandits or rebels. Their claim was similar to a *bona fide possessor.* The element of scandal must have been absent entirely in this case.

Gasparri's commentary on this response [18a]

"eadem repetas, si dubitetur num prius matrimonium validum fuerit,"

would indicate that the impediment of *ligamen* is primarily a matter of fact, namely, a matter of existence. In similar cases, capture among bandits, would incline the mind more towards presumed death of the one party than continued existence. The response of the Holy Office to the second case would strengthen this view without declaring definitely that the death could be presumed. This response was given also before the famous instruction of 1868 which contained the procedure for presuming death of one party who had disappeared.

[18] S.C.S. Off. (Nankin.), 22 mart., 1865,—*Fontes,* n. 982.

[18a] Gasparri, *De Matrimonio,* I, 349.

On a previous page Gasparri [18b] mentions plainly

> ". . . sed requiritur moralis certitudo, nam quis praesumitur vivere donec mors probetur et in dubio nemini coniugum debet praeiudicium ferri in iure suo ac novum matrimonium exponi periculo nullitatis."

It would hardly seem plausible that this eminent scholar and canonist had contradicted himself, in one case giving a rule to maintain a doubt and on a previous occasion advancing a method to depose it.

Another consideration in this procedure is that practically all the responses and rules advanced are to prevent those contemplating a second union from rushing into a possibly invalid marriage. Hence, the conjecture would easily be made that while the fact of the first marriage is established the second one would be invalid unless a situation arose indicative of death as in the response of the Holy Office of March 22, 1865. Consequently, mere absence would be no foundation on which to base a presumption of death or freedom from *ligamen.* Direct testimony is the most desirable; but indications and circumstances—in other words, well-founded presumptions—could also be introduced to establish proof of the demise of one spouse. This rule is most obvious in the instruction to the Bishops of the Oriental Rite [18c] and in a later answer of the Holy Office of 1891.[18d] Abstractly the viewpoint could be that once the first marriage is established the adjudication of the second marriage is identical with declaring officially whether the parties now living in a possibly invalid union are really *personae habiles* for a second marriage. Therefore, the same rules would be applied for those contemplating marriage as well as those who illicitly entered upon another contract.

If invalidity of the first marriage can be demonstrated the question of the death of one party does not come into consideration.

[18b] *De Matrimonio,* I, 346.

[18c] S. C. S. Off., instr. (ad Ep. Rituum Orient.), a. 1883, -*Fontes,* n. 1076.

[18d] S. C. S. Off., 8 maii 1891, -*Fontes,* n. 1135.

This particular phase of the subject is frequently overlooked in adjudicating a second marriage after the fact of a first marriage has been established. Unquestionably, it is the duty of the Defensor Vinculi to maintain the validity of the second marriage when it is brought before a tribunal for adjudication as to nullity. If the first marriage is established his objections that the first marriage may be invalid are worthless in so far as he would lead the court to believe that the presumption of the validity of the second marriage by reason of Canon 1014 is on his side and that he is relieved of the burden of proof. In the first place he has Canon 1069 § 2 against him, and secondly, by taking exception in this matter he becomes the actor in the trial and must prove his allegations. Furthermore, the statement coming from the Ordinary, *i. e.*, the result of a summary or extrajudicial investigation that a former marriage is still in existence obviates the possibility of going any further. The impediment of ligamen is present and the lack of the impediment is what would make the second marriage valid. *"Prior tempore, potior iure,"* is not unsound logic.

By reason of Canon 1971 the Promoter of Justice would attack the second marriage under consideration because the impediment is of a public nature. He would admit that ligamen arises from a valid marriage; two things arise, then, the fact of marriage and the validity. In accusing the second marriage the Promoter of Justice forces the parties of this union to prove that they had been free to contract this second marriage. Now, the fact of a first marriage of one of the parties is established with no indication of dissolution. This is sufficient for the full value of Canon 1014 to go into effect in favor of the Promoter of Justice along with the prohibition of Canon 1069 § 2. The validity of the first marriage is presumed and it is the burden of any one who claims it is not valid or that it is doubtful to show cause that the first marriage is invalid. If the Defensor Vinculi should in this fashion object or raise a doubt as to the validity of the first marriage it is his duty to PROVE his claims, *i. e.*, he must prove that the first marriage is positively invalid. It would not suffice if he established a doubt about the validity, for this doubt does not eliminate the presumption of law in favor of the first marriage. Canon 1014 explicitly states: "**Matrimonium gaudet favore iuris; quare in dubio standum est pro valore matrimonii, donec contrarium probetur, salvo praescripto can. 1127.**" Canon 1827 indicates the operation: "**Qui habet pro se iuris praesumptionem, liberatur ab onere probandi, quod recidit in partem adversam; qua non probante, sententia ferri debet in favorem partis pro qua stat praesumptio.**"

Of the various instructions that have come from the Holy See in reference to presumed death two carry rather detailed directions as to what indications would assist in determining death with moral certainty to a degree to allow a bishop to declare that the person who would otherwise be deprived of marriage may now enter another union. The Instruction of the Holy Office given May 13, 1868 was for this particular purpose only.[19] The Instruction of the Holy Office of 1883 to the Bishops of the Oriental Rite is in reference to investigations of marriage cases in general, but carries a detailed process on the method of establishing presumed death, also, in §§ 42 and 43 of Article 4 *De impedimento ligaminis*.[20] Both concur as to the same indications and methods of employing presumptions. The main argument to overcome is that no duration of time of absence suffices on which to found an argument in favor of death, even should this reason be advanced by the civil authorities as a sufficient cause. Otherwise any means that is ordinarily used to produce moral certitude is admitted.

In the use of the presumptions it would be of advantage to set up first the reason for leaving home and a cause that might bring about death. The next consideration would be to investigate the conditions before the subject left home and finally what the relations were between man and wife after the departure of the one under consideration.

The cause that is frequently advanced in this type of case is war or shipwreck. It is readily understood that the fact of enlisting in the government's active warfare would not be sufficient. Had the

[19] S.C.S. Off., instr. a. 1868,—*Fontes* n. 1002; cf. *Conc. Balt. Plen. III*, Appendix p. 258.

[20] S.C.S. Off., instr. (ad Ep. Rituum Orient.), a. 1883,—*Fontes* n. 1076.

person engaged in a particular battle in which all the men or the major part of them were slain there would be reason to attach credibility to such a situation being a cause of the death. The Holy See has from time to time given instructions and directions how to carry on the investigations for particular events.[21] Similar instructions have also been given for catastrophies, either of a natural or unusual order, as revolutions.[22] In the case of earthquakes the Holy See gave more serious instructions and did not grant general dispensations, but insisted that each case had to be investigated. A less serious investigation was permitted in the instance of men who had gone into battle and had not returned.[23] Every means of discovering information as to the actual participation of such an individual in a battle, revolution, shipwreck, or catastrophies would be of assistance in gaining knowledge of the truth. The bureaux of vital statistics, the rosters of the army or boats and the names as recorded of rescues, prisoners, refugees could be used as adminicular proof. Most important, however, would be to note seriously the reason and the occasion of the person going to war, or making a journey by water, or by rail, or by air. If one party left without knowledge of the other and only after quarrels and differences at home the testimony of the party seeking the declaration of presumed death would not be beyond suspicion.

The circumstances and indications antedating such an event would have to be gathered from the character of the person who had disappeared, from his habits, customs, possessions, in particular home and business, good or bad relations with his wife, children, or relatives, his business associations as to his honesty, liabilities and obligations; in general every indication that would give rise to the belief that the individual would rather be at home or away from home are to be weighed and considered.

In much the same fashion circumstances after the departure of the person would produce the same indications. Correspondence

[21] S.C.S. Off., July 22, 1898, after the battle of Adona; S.C. de Sacramentis, Dec. 16, 1910, after the Russian-Japanese war.

[22] S.C. de Sacramentis, March 12, 1910, after the earthquake in Messina, Sicily; S.C. Inq. 18/20 July, 1900, after the Revolution in Cuba. Cf. Ludwig Kaas, *Kriegsverschollenheit und Wiederherheiratung* (Paderborn, 1919), pp. 105-112.

[23] Cf. Chelodi, *Ius Matrimoniale*, p. 77; Knecht, *Handbuch des Katholischen Eherechts*, p. 382.

should be given particular consideration as to whether the party had given any external indication of intention to return. The condition of health, age, and occupation in a foreign land and the general hygiene of the territory as to the possibility of pestilence and local fatal diseases would point to possible solutions either for or against. The habits, customs, associations, and business of the person in a foreign land could be investigated. His reputation could be given special attention. Rumor as to the possible demise could also be used if supported by sufficient adminicular proof and the testimony of unimpeachable witnesses who had heard of the death either in or from the distant country. In the latter event the witnesses must be examined carefully to avoid possible collusion between them and the one seeking the declaration of death. If any doubt should arise as to their veracity their testimony would be of no value.

The instruction goes on to say that the daily papers should not be neglected in attempting to locate the person and also to establish the news of his death or whereabouts. Finally it must be noted that no single presumption would be conclusive, but the collection and intimate relation of facts and the circumstances viewed in their entirety in the absence of witnesses to the death could produce moral certainty, that is, beyond a reasonable doubt.

If the doubt should still persist and the case becomes involved recourse to the Holy See is permitted. All the *acts* of the investigation should be sent in or at least a good exposition of the case. A striking statement is made in reference to the *mors praesumpta* procedure in the instruction to the Bishops of the Oriental Rite about correspondence. The provision says in effect that if a regular practice of correspondence had been in force with the other spouse or at least communication by means of messengers and the communications should suddenly cease without any special cause a serious presumption would arise about the person's death.[24]

[24] A case of this nature is recorded in AAS., XIV, (1922), 96. Cf. S.C.S. Off., instr. 21 Aug., 1670,—*Fontes,* n. 742; S.C.S. Off. (Nankin.), 22 mart., 1865,—*Fontes,* n. 982; S.C.S. Off., instr. a. 1868,—*Fontes,* n. 1002; S.C.S. Off., instr. (ad Deleg. Ap. Aegyp), 13 ian., 1869;—*Fontes,* n. 1008; S.C.S. Off., instr. (ad Ep. Rituum Orient.), a. 1883,—*Fontes,* n. 1076; S.C.S. Off., instr. (ad Ep. Orient.), 22 Aug., 1890,—*Fontes,* n. 1128; S.C.S. Off., 8 maii, 1891,—*Fontes,* n. 1135; Gasparri, *De Matrimonio,* I, 346-349; W. Ursprung, *Verschollenheits- und Todeserklaerung* (AARAU, 1918).

CHAPTER II

CANON 1015

Canon 1015, § 2. Celebrato matrimonio, si coniuges simul cohabitaverint, praesumitur consummatio, donec contrarium probetur.

After the marriage once the parties cohabit consummation is presumed by law until the contrary is demonstrated.

By its nature and wording this Canon proposes a presumption of law. Its purpose in this particular section is to establish the difference between a simple *matrimonium ratum* and one *ratum et consummatum,* since different juridical effects follow in the two instances. However, a *matrimonium ratum* is in every degree just as valid a marriage even when not consummated. Consummation of marriage consists in the first complete act of marital intercourse between husband and wife after the marriage ceremony.[1] Cohabitation then is the so-called cause of this presumption of consummation. Since this is a *praesumptio iuris tantum* it will permit of proof to the contrary.

By cohabitation the custom in vogue in the country in which the marriage takes place must be given consideration. In the United States the honey-moon trip or the fact that the parties registered at a hotel would be sufficient evidence of cohabitation. It would imply, then, common life under normal circumstances, of bed or bed-chamber, board, or dwelling together for as short a time as one night. By reason of Canons 1111 and 1128, this constitutes a mutual right and the very nature of marriage as a contract for the rearing of offspring demands mutual dwelling and association. Triebs' reference[2] to

[1] A wider purpose of this presumption is evidently to obviate the anguish of physical examination as in the presumption of puberty. C. 5, C. XXVII, q. 2: ". . . Non defloratio virginitatis facit coniugium sed pactio coniugalis . . ." C. 5, X, *De Bigamis Non Ordinandis,* 1, 21; [c. 1] C. XXVII, q. 2: Matrimonium non facit coitus, sed voluntas."

[2] Triebs, *Handbuch des Kanonischen Eherechts* (Breslau, 1932, Ostdeutsche Verlagsanstalt), IV, p. 660.

consummation at the first opportunity after the celebration would require some qualification. Experience and the nature of the union all tend to infer as much, but tribal customs could be adverse to such a conclusion. The sole fact, too, that the bridal couple were alone for a few hours apart from the public eye could hardly constitute cohabitation. Other circumstances of time and place would have to be injected.[3]

Westermarck records that among the Huron Indians it was customary for young married people to cohabit for one year as brother and sister to prove that they had higher ideals in marrying than simply gratification of sex. The Tlingit tribe of Indians in Alaska had a custom of not consummating marriage for four weeks after the ceremony.[4]

The tenor of the law would seem to be that it would be necessary for man and wife to give some evidence of having established common life (normally for one night), by occasion and means indicative of or affording the opportunity for the *unio carnis*. In the Decisions of the Rota regarding impotence the strength of the presumption of consummation after cohabitation may be gained from the preponderance of testimony required in establishing proofs of impotence, especially by the physical examination of qualified physicians to establish virginity. Also, in cases of affinity as a diriment impediment in the former legislation, the testimony of witnesses declaring illicit associations of the two parties ranging from eye witnessing of the sin itself down a complete gamut to the moral inclinations and propensities of the two people concerned was admitted. Any indications of gifts, journeys, visits to the home or hotel room (even during the daytime), reputation, overheard conversations build up a strong presumption of illicit association. The same arguments can obviously be used to presume consummation in marriage today.[5]

In regard to consummation authors are very much at variance as to what acts would fulfill the requirements of the law.[6] Consum-

[3] Tobias, VI, 17-18.

[4] Edward Westermarck, *The History of Human Marriage* (London, 1906), II, 559-563; Knecht, *Handbuch des Kath. Eherechts*, p. 41.

[5] S. R. Rotae Decisiones, XIV (1922), 245-252.

[6] Gasparri covers this matter thoroughly in discussing impotence. Gasparri, *De Matrimonio* (ed. 1932), II, p. 329.

mation is primarily a human act, *i. e.*, an act of the will, but it is also, an act of nature. Provided all the physical requirements are present the presumption would always be invoked. To attempt after cohabitation to prove non-consummation would demand convincing proof in establishing moral certitude, at least. Physical examination, testimony of physicians in reference to sickness or disease, illicit contracts as to abuse of marriage and their consequences could, if conclusively established, overthrow the presumption. The same may be said of circumstances such as scruples over lack of consent, force or induced fear, or the particular aversion for such actions, especially on the part of the woman. Such indications could give rise to valid inferences to outweigh the provisions of the law.[7] In reference to the physical requirements for consummation the opinion of Gasparri seems to be the more prevalent view, *i. e.*, penetratio membri virilis in vaginam et effusio veri seminis in eadem. The *potestas coeundi* is all that is required. The *potestas generandi* is an added faculty of nature, the absence of which is no impediment.[8] With this view the full requirement of Canon 1081, § 2 "actus per se aptos ad prolis generationem" would obtain. Onanism or sodomy would not constitute consummation. Neither would so-called artificial fecundation (test-tube babies) or an imperfect act of intercourse suffice for consummation in spite of the fact of a subsequent pregnancy. However, in any such case the presumption of law would hold until juridical proofs establish the contrary.[9]

In the Regulae Servandae of 1923 for cases submitted for a dispensation *super matrimonio rato et non consummato* [10] chapter XII mentions the following as causes indicative of non-consummation: (a) lack of consent on the part of the man; (b) force and fear; (c) aversion and hatred between the spouses from the beginning of

[7] Reg. Servandae in Processibus super rato (1923) caput XII #80. AAS, XV (1923).

[8] Gasparri, *De Matrimonio,* §§ 509, 515, 516. S.R. Rotae Decisiones, Vol. XIV (1922), p. 281, § 11.

[9] The Holy Office forbade artificial fecundation on March 17, 1897. Cf. ASS, XXIX, 704; Triebs, *Handbuch des Kanonischen Eherechts,* IV, 657; Wernz-Vidal, *Ius Canonicum* (Romae, 1928), V, p. 18 & 19.

[10] Reg. Servandae (1923), Super Rato, A.A.S., XV (1923).

married life; (d) impotence, either absolute or relative.[11] While it can not be said with any degree of certainty that non-consummation would obtain in any of these cases, nevertheless, the circumstances preceding and following a wedding would aid in determining the non-consummation from the cause alleged. The same procedure requires the *testes septimae manus* who must testify to the character and truthfulness of the statements of the parties. Their testimony, however, is only adminicular proof since it pertains only to credibility not to the fact itself.

Other witnesses may be introduced to testify as to agreements, the type of fear, or the conditions under which consummation might have been completed. Members of the household, immediate family, and servants can advance valuable testimony to overthrow the force of the law.[12]

[11] Cf. S. R. Rotae Decisiones XIV (1922), p. 111; p. 153; p. 231; p. 241; p. 291; p. 311.

[12] S. R. Rotae Decisiones III (1911), p. 234; p. 350-351.

CHAPTER III

CANON 1082

> **Canon 1082, § 1. Ut matrimonialis consensus haberi possit, necesse est ut contrahentes saltem non ignorent matrimonium esse societatem permanentem inter virum et mulierem ad filios procreandos.**
>
> **§ 2. Haec ignorantia post pubertatem non praesumitur.**
>
> **§ 1. That the matrimonial consent obtain, it is necessary that the contracting parties are at least not ignorant of the fact that matrimony is a permanent institution between a man and a woman for the procreation of children.**
>
> **§ 2. This ignorance is not presumed after puberty has been reached.[1]**

The pivotal point of paragraph one is ". . . societatem permaentem inter virum et mulierem ad filios procreandos." In paragraph two the legislation presumes that there is no one of the physical age for marriage who is ignorant of the nature of this union. It is a presumption of law and admits proof to the contrary.

Puberty in Canon Law is the presumed physical maturity once a definite age has been reached. According to Canon 88, § 2 the age is 14 years for males, and 12 years for females. It was believed in Roman Law that physical maturity went hand in hand with mental maturity, hence, marriage was permitted for those who showed a definite age has been reached. According to Canon 88 § 2 the the first signs of the physical capability of reproduction. It was Justinian who introduced the presumption of puberty with a legal age to avoid the necessity of physical examination.[2] However, for

[1] A liberty has been taken in the translation with the expression "non ignorent" for the purpose of explaining the "ignorantia" of paragraph 2.

[2] Chelodi, *Ius Matrimoniale,* p. 66-67; Freisen, *Canonische Eherecht,* pp. 323-324.

marriage the Code has extended the required age to sixteen years for boys and fourteen years for girls.[3]

Since marriage is a contract as well as a sacrament it must give rise to rights and obligations. The object, then, of the contract will be the matter with which the consent is ultimately concerned. The definition of marriage as laid down in the Code (Canon 1081 § 2), "Consensus matrimonialis est actus voluntatis quo utraque pars tradit et acceptat ius in corpus, perpetuum et exclusivum, in ordine ad actus per se aptos ad prolis generationem," must be considered.

The Canon under discussion qualifies the knowledge of "actus per se aptos ad prolis generationem." The law is not concerned how this knowledge is acquired. Chelodi [4] says "natura duce haec discimus," but since there is no infused knowledge this matter must be communicated to us by instruction or experience. It is not known by intuition as is obvious from experience. The law further allows that such cases may arise and in the event that they do those who allege ignorance are burdened with the full proof.

The Canon states only negatively the amount or degree of knowledge required for the consent. It would give rise to the following questions:

1) Is the knowledge of a "societas permanens inter virum et mulierem ad filios procreandos" required for a valid marriage?

2) Is this concept of the "societas permanens etc.," identical with the knowledge of the requirement of the "copula carnalis?"

3) Would lack of knowledge of the copula alone exclude the consent?

Ad. 1. Unquestionably, if consent is given and the notion of procreation is excluded willingly or through complete ignorance the marriage is invalid.[5] A case may arise where someone believes marriage to be a friendly relationship where two people may serve one another permanently without the knowledge of the purpose of rearing children. This excludes one of the essentials of marriage, the ***bonum prolis.***

Ad. 2. From the wording of the Canon 1082 § 1 it is difficult to

[3] Canon 1067 § 1.

[4] Chelodi, *Ius Matrimoniale,* p. 119.

[5] Vermeersch-Creusen, *Epitome* (1925), II, p. 216.

say definitely what the societas permanens means and whether the phrase "ad filios procreandos" comprehends knowledge of the copula or not.

The presumption rests negatively on the fact of physical maturity. The moment the twelfth or fourteenth birthday arrives ignorance on sex life in marriage is no longer presumed. Before this moment the law does presume ignorance.

The further removed a person is in age after puberty the stronger would be the presumption for absence of ignorance, whereas proximity would weaken, but not remove, the presumption. The fact of consummation also bears on the allegation. Both these considerations seem to be the determining factors in three cases submitted to the Holy See.

In the case of Ventimilien [6] the girl was only twelve years and nine months old. The Acta reveal that she was minutely questioned about consummation which was proved not to have taken place. However, the marriage was annulled on the score of ignorance. The demeanor, mental development and general appearance in dress and manner indicated a child-like mind sufficiently to incline one to believe the girl was ignorant of the duties of marriage.

In the Bamberg case [7] non-consummation was proved and in spite of this fact after three distinct and conformable sentences were passed the marriage was not annulled on the grounds of ignorance because the actrix was 22 years old.

In a case judged by the Rota in 1910 [8] the actrix was also 22 years old when she contracted marriage. Against her will the marriage was consummated. The entire presentation of the case demonstrates quite clearly the operation of the presumption under discussion. Nowhere does the testimony show that the girl had sufficient knowledge to marry. On the contrary it does show that she failed to convince the court that she was ignorant to the extent to declare the marriage null. While her two brothers testified that their mother had not instructed the children in sex matters the possibility of the

[6] S.C.C., in Ventimilien., Matrimonii, May 19, 1888—Thesaurus (1888), pp. 289-350.

[7] S.C.C., Bambergensi—Matrimonii, March 14, 1856.

[8] S.R. Rotae Decisiones, II (1910), pp. 112-122.

girl having been instructed privately was not excluded. Secondly, the pastor had read a marriage instruction to the future bride from a book. No matter how little enlightenment the reading may have given there would be a strong presumption against ignorance after an instruction. Thirdly, the actrix in her own testimony did not so much allege ignorance but rather showed that she abhorred the notion of sexual relations and had a positive will opposed to its fulfillment.

Authors seem to be at a loss to declare when ignorance is présent or as some attempt to say how little knowledge is required. All agree that a knowledge of the copula is not required. Gasparri seems to dissociate the concepts of *societas* and *procreatio* as a *status* and a *modus*, but concludes that if both know that *vir ex uxore filios procreat* in this *societas* the consent is valid.[9]

Chelodi uses much of the same terminology, but is not definitely clear. He avers that if two people enter marriage in the same way as others do the consent implies all duties and obligations. The least he maintains they must know is that virum *ex uxore* filios procreare (italics, Chelodi).[10]

Vermeersch-Creusen allows that the couple should know at least that by bodily contact a child is obtained and is born by the mother.[11] This view would obtain if the traditio iuris were erroneously considered only as oscula, amplexus, familiaritas sine copula. Ayrinhac-Lydon claim that to enter marriage believing that children are begotten per oscula is invalid in the opinion of some authors.[12]

The Decision of the Rota mentioned previously seems to require very little.

> ". . . ut contractus quivis validus sit (maxime si non unam tantum obligationem contineat) non exigitur ut singula officia et obligationes cognoscant contrahentes, quae ex ipso contractu derivant, sed satis est ut voluntas contrahen-

[9] Gasparri, *De Matrimonio*, II, p. 27.

[10] Chelodi, *Ius Matrimoniale*, p. 119.

[11] Vermeersch-Creusen, *Epitome*, II, p. 216; cf. Capello, *De Matrimonio*, n. 582; Vlaming, *Praelectiones*, II, 523; Wernz-Vidal, *Ius Canonicum*, V, 547.

[12] Ayrinhac-Lydon, *Marriage Legislation in the New Code of Canon Law*, p. 195; Capello, n. 582.

> tium feratur in contractum, universim sumptum, prout ab aliis frequentari consueverit." Ita etiam sentit Rosset, *De Sacr. Matr. n. 837:* "Sufficit ad valorem contractus matrimonii, ut contrahens noscat consortium individuae vitae per matrimonium instituendum atque modo confuso apprehendat illud consortium esse institutum ad filios generandos, quin noverit ea, quae spectant ad naturam modumque generationis" cui doctrinae adstipulatur etiam La Croix, *Theol. mor., lib. 6, tract. 6, de matr. n. 556:* "Si virgo putavit commixtionem corporum non esse necessariam ad generandam prolem, valide contraxit, quia habuit generalem intentionem faciendi quod alii contrahentes faciunt. Gobat n. 128." [13]

Vlaming insists that the parties must know children are born by means of the cupola for valid consent.[14] While Chelodi does not say the same he infers that Vlaming's argument is worthy of consideration.[15] Knecht follows the same line of thought.[16] They say, in effect, that in marriage as in other contracts the purpose or purposes of the contract must be willed and known. The right that is transferred must consist in the right to use the body of each other for the purpose of procreating children. "How can anyone validly transfer this power if he is ignorant of its objective purpose?" asks Vlaming.

It must be noted that this assertion puts ignorance in the same class as error. Effectively, however, in this regard they would be identical. Hence, whoever can prove that ignorance of the copula carnalis actually existed in the moment consent was given certainly did not intend to enter "in contractum universim sumptum prout ab aliis frequentari consueverit." Such a person was in error.[17] To the second question, then, "Is this concept of the societas permanens identical with the knowledge of the requirement of the "copula carnalis" the answer is no. However, from the use of the words in

[13] S.R. Rotae, Decisiones, II, p. 117 sqq.

[14] Vlaming, *Praelectiones*, II, n. 524.

[15] Chelodi, *Ius Matrimoniale*, p. 119.

[16] Knecht, *Handbuch des Katholischen Eherechts*, p. 548.

[17] *A S S* 5, 554; Knecht, *Handbuch des Katholischen Eherechts*, p. 548; Chelodi, *Ius Matrimoniale*, p. 119.

Canon 1082 of "societas . . . inter virum et mulierem," "procreandi," "post pubertatem," and in Canon 1081 of "tradere ius in corpus . . . ad actus aptos ad prolis generationem" the lack of some hazy knowledge of the purpose of the generative faculties in marriage would have to be demonstrated by anyone who alleges ignorance and that this ignorance existed at the time the consent was given.

A more precise statement can hardly be made. Nor can any more information be gathered from the praxis of the Holy See. With the exception of the case of Ventimilien where ignorance was conclusively proved the other cases always exhibit, not the presence of ignorance, but an intention opposed to the conjugal act.

Ad. 3. From the foregoing it must be concluded that lack of knowledge of the copula alone does not vitiate the consent. The Sacred Congregation of the Council gave a decision to this effect in 1870.[18] It has been the constant teaching of the Church since the time of the Decretals that "Nuptias facit consensus, non concubitus."[19] The knowledge would not refer to the modus of the societas permanens but to the general principle. Should one party refuse to render the debitum he or she might be enlightened. The consent would necessarily have to be renewed at least privately. If consummation is effected by violence the party that still persists in the error may introduce a cause for declaration of nullity; if one continues to refuse to submit a suit may be introduced *super rato et non consummato*. The evidence to subvert the presumption of law in Canon 1082 would have to be quite strong.

It must be noted that nowhere does the Canon use the words "scire," or "cognoscere," or "debita cognitio," or the like. The Canon does not say 'Haec scientia praesumitur" but "Haec ignorantia non praesumitur." Obviously it is a statement of the presumption of law with the consequence of shifting the burden of proof. It was necessary to use ignorantia, because "non ignorent" was employed in paragraph one. "Non ignoro" in Latin would be a strengthening form of "scio" or "cognosco." Since the clause "societas permanens"

[18] A S S, V, 554: "Matrimonium validum esse, quamquam aliquis ex coniugibus postea ignorasse se dicat matrimoniale debitum eoque cognito non fuisse matrimonium initurum affirmet."

[19] Knecht, *Handbuch des Katholischen Eherechts*, p. 546, n. 2.

is indeterminate it must have been in the mind of the legislator to indicate that should even this slight idea of married life not be known the parties would be similar to those before puberty who are presumed to lack the required knowledge for marital consent.

Strangely enough authors,[20] a Decision of the Rota, and the Sacred Congregation of the Council use "scientia." [21] These decisions were made before the Code, but the jurisprudence of the cases is no different from the present day. There seems to be another hidden reason for the insertion of the word "ignorantia." Invariably in cases of this type the strongest argument would be "had I known such matters before marriage, I would never have married." If this is real error there is lack of sufficient discretion, but it is not to be presumed. The absence of such knowledge must be proved. To allow for an evident change of mind is contrary to the nature of a contract, especially in marriage since it is a permanent institution. Such an hypothesis is an empty one, a plain "if—" for the future, and has no foundation, consequently, does not exist. It usually arises post factum and has no real corresponding antecedent. The act of the will under such circumstances is called interpretative and is negligible in an allegation. The intention in the will must be actual, real, and accompany the action; or, it may be virtual, habitual, *i. e.*, given previously and never revoked.[22]

[20] Gasparri, *De Matrimonio,* II, p. 13, "discretio mentis"; Chelodi, *Ius Matrimoniale,* p. 119; Wernz-Vidal, *Ius Canonicum,* V, 547; Ayrinhac-Lydon, *Marriage Legislation,* p. 194.

[21] S.R. Rotae Decisiones, II (1910), Dec. XII, n. 2 & 6; Knecht, *Handbuch des Katholischen Eherechts,* p. 547, n. 4; S.C.C. June 15, and May 19, 1888 in A S S, XXI, 180.

[22] The usual observation made by the authors in regard to the interpretative will is simply to say that the error gives rise to the cause and to offer no further explanation. Salsmans interpretation in this regard is most pertinent. ". . . Quid autem est 'error dans causam?' In hoc quidam errant simpliciter ponentes: Error dedit causam, si quis sincere dicat, veritatem agnoscens: "Si hoc scivissem, non contraxissem." Si enim nullo modo de hac re cogitavit, neque ullum errorem circa eam habuit. Nam ut sit error, oportet saltem confuse eliciatur iudicium erroneum. Unde si de circumstantia satis extraordinaria vel extranea agitur, quae tamen cognita vel supposita retinuisset a contrahendo, sed nullatenus in mente versabatur, nemo sapiens dixerit contractum esse initum ex errore dante causam . . ." "Circa vitia consensus," J. Salsmans, *Jus Pontificium,* X (1930), 104-109; Gasparri, *De Matrinomio* II, 11; Chelodi, *Ius Matrimoniale,* p. 119.

In connection with this matter of "ignorantia" it is well to take note of an old *Regula Iuris* of Boniface VIII, *"Praesumitur ignorantia, ubi scientia non probatur."* [23] While this rule is applied by the law and by authors in conditions where neighbors or relatives are presumed to know local affairs and events [24] or that in small localities the happenings are presumed more public than occult, nevertheless, it seems reasonable that by placing the converse in the Code of Canon Law the legislator could prevent anyone from invoking this old and established rule even in such matters as sufficient knowledge for marriage. Consequently, the total burden of proof is on the plaintiff. Neither the defendant, nor the court, need prove that any knowledge existed.

It would be far easier for the plaintiff to disprove the required knowledge than to show an utter lack of it. In this form the presumption operates more forcibly since the contention of the plaintiff is founded on a negative fact—ignorance (Carentia debitae cognitionis).

It is in connection with Canons 1081 and 1082 that insanity causes are judged. The application of presumptions of man are the basis for the sentence.[25]

Since every man is presumed to be mentally normal by nature, the insanity must be proved; it is not presumed. In Volume XIV of the Rota Decisions Causa XXXIV #3 the principle is rendered as follows:

> "Ad irritandum matrimonium ex capite amentiae, nempe, requiritur et sufficit ut, momento quo contractum est, nupturiens mente captus fuerit, seu rationis usum non habuerit

[23] R. J., 45 in VI°; cf. Canon 15.

[24] C. 7 & 8, X, *De Praesumptionibus,* II, 23. Reiffenstuel, *Ius Can. Univ.,* II, XXIII, 108 & 109. Menochius, *De Praesumptionibus,* VI, 24.

[25] S.R. Rotae Decisiones, XIV (1922), Dec. XXXIV, p. 313. In reference to insanity Menochius, *De Praesumptionibus,* VI, 45, 18, says "Quae sane sententia probatur . . . . et ratione, nempe, quod natura ipsa parit homines sanae mentis: et ideo qui asserit aliquem esse insanem repugnat ipsi naturae, atque ita ei adversatur praesumptio, quae a natura ipsa descendit. Et quae quidem praesumptio eum probationis onere gravat." VI, 45, 22. "Cum ergo is qui asserit aliquem esse furiosum vel dementem, teneatur furorem et dementiam probare, ea poterit coniecturis seu signis, et praesumptionibus, quae eam inserunt, probari."

> ad substantiam matrimonialis contractus intelligendam. Si autem ante et post illud tempus indubia dederit signa habitualis amentiae, praesumitur, donec contrarium probetur, contrahentem etiam medio tempore, seu in matrimonio contrahendo, amentem fuisse."

The decision rendered in this case was favorable on the grounds that when a person has been declared insane by experts both before and after the time marriage was contracted, he is presumed to have been insane at the moment of the contract, also, because insanity is by its nature a permanent disease. Neither are lucid intervals presumed. Should they arise they are considered accidental and, consequently negligible.[26] The presumption employed in insanity cases is that there is a lack of free will and sufficient power of discretion to perform a human act. Matrimonial consent demands both, an act of the will and an act of the intellect.

[26] S.R. Rotae Decisiones, I (1909), p. 92; Gasparri, *Matrimonio,* II, 14.

CHAPTER IV

CANON 1086 § 1

Can. 1086 § 1. "Internus animi consensus semper praesumitur conformis verbis vel signis in celebrando matrimonio adhibitis."

§ 1. "The internal consent of the will is presumed to conform to the words and signs employed in celebrating marriage."

Because marriage is a contract the essential part consists in mutual consent of the contracting parties. The manifestation should be made in the best means at the disposal of human beings. The ordinary means is words expressing the transition of rights. For those unable to speak, signs or writing are permitted. External expression with any significant sign, such as giving and accepting the ring would suffice for validity.[1]

The presumption as mentioned in the Canon is one of law, but the underlying principle is an ordinary presumption of human experience. Ordinarily people are taken at their word, and their words and expressions are given the normal interpretation of the language in use at the time. To deny an accepted interpretation of words employed or the obligations incumbent upon the wording of the contract immediately involves a contradiction. To assert something and not mean what is said is to venture two acts of the will at one and the same moment, hence simulation.[2]

In marriage the consent expresses an exchange of rights and the corresponding obligations to respect these rights. To give external

[1] Thomas Sanchez, *De Sancto Matrimonii Sacramento Disputationum*, (Lugduni, 1669), I, 8, 12.

[2] "Verum enim est cum dicitur esse quod est, vel non esse quod non est. Falsum autem est cum dicitur non esse quod est, vel esse quod non est."—St. Thomas, Met. IV, L. 8.

expression to will the exchange and at the same time to will not to give the rights vitiates the act.

Since consent is an act of the will it must have the all essential quality of a human action, i. e., it must be free. While it is a mutual contract involving another person's rights it must be an honest expression of inward intention. Because consent deals with a contract peculiar to marriage it must be unconditional in reference to past and present.

In reference to the object of marriage the consent must be an act of the will to effect a contract with all the obligations essential to the contract, namely, marriage itself and all its constitutive parts. If any of the conditions of the act of the will are absent or caused to be absent the consent is vitiated and the contract void.

The consent may be affected either extraneously or interiorly to destroy its binding force. Fear or coercion could violate the freedom of the act. Conditions, specifically made or implied, as through error or ignorance, would affect the consent interiorly. A positive act of the will contrary to the consent as given would be simulation.[3]

If these two acts of the will are contradictory only one can be carried out. It is not psychologically possible to act and not act, to consent and not consent at the same time. Neither is it correct to say that since two intentions are contradictory they eliminate or destroy each other. It is a question of which intention is the prevailing one. Those who witnessed the external act must necessarily conclude that this act was the *intentio praevalens*. However, an antecedent and opposite intention, and the corresponding fulfillment of this intention, would lead us to the conclusion that the antecedent intention was more prevalent at the time its very opposite was placed in evidence.

Since simulation is an internal act unless the intention were previously known, it can only be demonstrated by presumptions *post factum*. There is a presumption of law against the plaintiff at the very start. It is impossible to explore the mental activity in another's mind without an exterior display in some perceptible form.

[3] F. Roberti, "Quaestiones quaedam de Identificatione Actionum ob vitia consensus in causis matrimonialibus," *Apollinaris*, VI, (1933), 105-107; D. 22, 3, 22. Ulpian,—"Eum, qui voluntatem mutatam dicit, probare hoc debere."

The confession of the simulating party even under oath would not constitute sufficient proof in foro externo since it would simply consist in a contradiction of the consent expressed. This is exactly what must be proved. To present the reason for the simulation would give a basis for estimating the circumstances before, during, and immediately after the marriage.[4] Canon 1086 §2 states further that besides fictitious consent the parties are not to make reservations without danger of rendering the marriage void by excluding marriage itself, all right to the conjugal act, or any essential property of marriage.

Simulation is somewhat different and carries the intention 1) not to marry, 2) to marry, but not to accept obligations of marriage, 3) to marry to accept the obligations, but not to fulfill them.[5]

Ad 1. To exclude marriage itself and accept it is contradictory, hence, the marriage is invalid. To prove this in foro externo the reason for the act must be presented, whether deception, lust, money, business-partnership, publicity (as with actresses) etc.; if the reason is established the estimation of acts and circumstances preceding, during, and following the marriage can be more readily interpreted and understood. The acts and circumstances can not be judged separately, but must be viewed in their entirety. A written agreement made before marriage (as for publicity) could be offered as proof of wrong intention, but it is also possible that the wrong intention could have been revoked either before the ceremony or in the actual placing of the consent itself.[6]

Should there be insufficient proof for the contention of the plaintiff, there would exist a conflict between the internal and external forum. If one insists that he feigned consent he is bound to live with the other party externally. In conscience he must abstain from all use of marriage since he knows he is living in an invalid union. The consent could be renewed privately in a manner to revoke the former agreement in order to make the marriage valid.

Ad 2. To marry, and exclude the obligations of marriage. Ac-

[4] Wernz-Vidal, *Ius Canonicum,* V, 551.

[5] Gasparri, *De Matrimonio,* II, 36, 814.

[6] Cf. S. R. Rotae Decisiones, Vol. 1 (1909), Dec. VIII, p. 72; Dec. XII, p. 106-107.

cording to Canon 1081 § 2 the obligations would arise from a) the "traditio et acceptatio iuris in corpus," b) "the ius perpetuum et exclusivum," c) "ad actus per se aptos ad prolis generationem." To elicit a positive act of the will to exclude any one or all three of these rights before the marriage or at one and the same time when the marriage consent is given would vitiate the consent and render the marriage null *ab initio*.[7] It would not be necessary to have any kind of agreement, written or oral, neither is it necessary that both parties will to exclude one of these three essentials. If only one should so act the marriage would redound to the same class as mentioned above. It would be equivalent to excluding marriage itself.[8] Where in the preceding Ad 1, marriage itself in its entirety was excluded by an opposite intention, in the second instance a distinction must be made.

The Decretum pro Armenis attributes to marriage the tria bona, i. e., sacramenti, fidei, prolis. The bonum sacramenti concerns itself with the indivisibility of the union, as Christ with the Church; the bonum fidei responds to the fidelity between the spouses; the bonum prolis refers to the procreation and education of children.[9] To violate the bonum sacramenti in marital consent would be equivalent to contracting a soluble marriage. If such is the intention of one or both of the contracting parties then the consent is not perpetual and exclusive as requested by Canons 1081 and 1086. To exclude one of the three bona of matrimony vitiates the consent since each of these three properties is essential. In regard to the execution of the three essentials the bonum sacramenti must be fulfilled; the bonum prolis and fidei can be abused without rendering the consent void. Consequently, for any person to give consent in marriage for a limited time is wrong. Companionate marriages are void for this

[7] Canon 1086 § 2.

[8] Cf. S. R. Rotae Decisiones, Vol. XIV (1922), Dec. X, pp. 84 & 85.

[9] Denzinger-Bannwart, *Enchyridion* (Friburg, 1911), #702, "Assignatur autem triplex bonum matrimonii. Primum est proles suscipienda et educanda ad cultum Dei. Secundum est fides, quam unus coniugum alteri servare debet. Tertium indivisibilitas matrimonii, propter hoc quod significat indivisibilem coniunctionem Christi et Ecclesiae. Quamvis autem ex causa fornicationis liceat tori separationem facere, non tamen aliud matrimonium contrahere fas est, cum matrimonii vinculum legitime contracti perpetuum sit."

reason. The same must be said of publicity marriages of stage and screen stars where each reserves the right to break the marriage for divorce *a vinculo* for the sake of front page notoriety.[10]

In general it would not be necessary to exclude these essentials by a positive intention to the contrary. The same effect may arise through error or ignorance. Due to the influence of education, religious training, or local custom a person may contract marriage considering it a soluble union.[11] The ignorance or error could be equivalent to an absolute condition contrary to the indissolubility.[12] The same reasoning would apply to positive intentions either contra bonum fidei or contra bonum prolis. They belong intimately to the ius matrimoniale in spite of the fact that both can be abused. Therefore, to marry with the intention *as a right* to maintain or have relations with mistresses or women other than a legitimate wife is contrary to the tradere-acceptare ius perpetuum et exclusivum.

The intention contra bonum prolis would have to be made in the same category. It is best to explain this intention in the treatment of the third class to follow.

Ad 3. To marry with the intention to accept the obligations of marriage and not fulfill them. The consent is the essential part of the marriage contract. Even before a marriage is consummated once the consent is expressed a real marriage is in effect. Coition completes the integrity, but does not add to the essence. The marriage exists after consent and before the copula, that is, that it is not necessary to exercise rights and privileges of marriage everyone agrees.

In reference to the fulfillment of these obligations Canonists apparently are of one mind that if these obligations are forsaken willingly for a higher purpose no consent is vitiated. The same authors admit, also, if after consent is given and rights transferred the parties intend to abuse marriage by acts "per se NON aptos

[10] Chelodi, *Ius Matrimoniale,* p. 127.

[11] S. C. Rotae Decisiones, V (1913), p. 178. The reference is to the famous Castellane-Gould case that was declared null for this very reason. This decision was later reversed. "En Amérique, presque toutes les jeunes filles, qui se marient, ont cette intention d'user du divorce, si le mariage ne les rend pas heureuses."

[12] Roberti, "Quaestiones quaedam de identificatione actionum ob vitia consensus in causis matrimonialibus," *Appollinaris,* VI (1933), 105-107.

ad generationem" the marriage consent is not vitiated.[13] Should, however, two people by a positive act of the will intend either jointly or separately not to fulfill all the obligations of marriage by abuse and at the same moment express the intention to oblige themselves to these obligations, they would seem to be uttering a contradiction. This, however, is not so. The consent given is genuine, but the will opposed to the fulfillment of obligations is no more than an agreement to sin. Nevertheless, it must be admitted that such an agreement may give rise to a condition *sine qua non* or a positive act of the will to exclude one of the three bona matrimonialia. Should this exclusion arise from a condition, error, ignorance, or a positive act of the will, the consent is vitiated and the contract is invalid *ab initio*. The question to be answered here is: is it possible to consent to marriage and at the same moment agree to sin against marriage? And the answer is, although it is grievously sinful, it is possible. The two acts do not contradict each other. They can co-exist. Whoever wishes an end must also use the means to that end.[14] In a decision of the Rota[15] an observation is made as to the difficulty of resolving a doubtful marriage contracted in error with fictitious consent. Naturally, the Court will adhere to Canon 1014 should the doubt remain and insist on the validity of the marriage. Still, a proof to overthrow the presumption is not impossible. If a reasonable cause is established that existed prior to the ceremony, and the circumstances both before, during, and after the ceremony showed a logical connection and relation consonant with the cause it may be presumed that in the placing of consent the more specific act contrary to Canon 1086 § 2, prevailed over the general intention to contract marriage as instituted by Christ.[16]

It has been the practice of authors and the Sacred Rota to indi-

[13] Wernz-Vidal, *Ius Can.* V. p. 552; Gasparri, *De Matrimonio,* II, p. 46.

[14] Cf. S. R. Rotae *Decisiones,* Vol. XIV, (1922) Dec. X, § 4, p. 87. Vermeersch-Creusen, *Epitome,* II, p. 218, § 374. The Rev. Bartholomew T. Timlin, O.F.M., in his work Conditional Matrimonial Consent (Washington, D. C.) (1934), presents a comprehensive discussion on this subject of conditions, errors, and will opposed to marriage between pages 215-340.

[15] S. R. Rotae *Decisiones* VII (1915), p. 292.

[16] S. R. Rotae *Decisiones* V (1913), p. 191-193. De Angelis, *Praelectiones Iuris Canonici* (Romae 1880), IV, 5, 7.

cate that the law in these latter cases presumes that the contracting parties agreed to abuse rather than exclude marriage. The Canon, 1082 § 1, does not so state, neither does it so infer. It is to be observed that a presumption of law is being enforced. If those who present a case for declaration of nullity allege consent was destroyed by a positive act of the will contra bonum prolis the law requires sufficient evidence to overthrow the legal presumption drawn from the fact and words of the ceremony. While in the majority of cases the fact of abuse of marriage may be easily demonstrated it is not so evident that the will was opposed to the essentials before or in the act of giving consent. Nor will the court presume from the evidence produced post factum that the exclusion of an obligation was present ante factum or in facto. The law stands on its presumption. The plaintiff must prove his allegations. In the event of insufficient proof or evidence the law does not presume the parties agreed to sin, but that the internal consent of the will as expressed in words or signs rendered the marriage valid.[17]

[17] Can. 1086 § 1; cf. Chelodi, *Ius Matrimoniale,* p. 127; S. R. Rotae, *Decisiones,* VI, 516; VII, 292.

CHAPTER V

CANON 1115

Can. 1115 § 1. "Pater is est quem iustae nuptiae demonstrant, nisi evidentibus argumentis contrarium probetur.

§ 2. Legitimi praesumuntur filii qui nati sunt saltem post sex menses a die celebrati matrimonii, vel intra decem menses a die dissolutae vitae coniugalis."

§ 1. The father is he whom lawful marriage indicates unless the contrary is proved by evident arguments.

§ 2. Children are presumed legitimate who are born at least six months from the day marriage is celebrated or within ten months from the day of dissolution of conjugal life.

Physically and naturally a mother of a child is easily known [1] but, doubt can be raised in regard to the father. Hence the principle enunciated in the first paragraph of this Canon. The principle and doctrine are taken bodily from Roman Law.

This is a legal presumption and will consequently give way to the truth. The direct object of the Canon is not to establish legitimacy, but paternity.

Father and son are correlative terms. In the filius there is indicated a *genitor* and a *genetrix* and the *suboles*. To demonstrate the genitor in the suboles is to prove simple procession as from cause to effect.

[1] D. 2, 4, 4 and 5: "Parentes etiam eos accipi Labeo existimat, qui in servitute susceperunt; nec tamen, ut Severus dicebat, ad solos iustos liberos, sed et si vulgo quaesitus sit filius, matrem in ius non vocabit, quia semper certa est, etiamsi vulgo conceperit; pater vero is est, quem nuptiae demonstrant."

This would signify a father—genitor—only in the natural order. Pater, or paternitas, in Canon 1115 is a wider concept. It comprises not only the fact of generation, but its consequences in rights and privileges, duties and obligations, honors and labors for the father, mother, and child. The law qualifies the word "Pater" with "iustae nuptiae," to infer that in the idea of the presumption an honest marriage gives rise to the legal concept of paternity.

Negatively the law, also, provides that this may not be the case (". . . nisi evidentibus argumentis contrarium probetur.") Fatherhood can exist without marriage. However, in this event the *pater* is not provided for by the terminology of the Canon, but must be pointed out by the evident truth (*evidentibus argumentis*). Should the truth not be established in the absence of *"iustae nuptiae"* the law offers no solution to acknowledging the father. Under such circumstances none of the consequences that flow from father to child could be invoked on the strength of this canon. But given the *iustae nuptiae* the law does point out the father, not by a scientific investigation, nor by intensive watchfulness over the actions of husband and wife once they have contracted marriage, but by the simple *presumptio iuris*.

The structure of this legal principle is founded on the normal sequence of events of everyday life, namely, marriage is an institution for the procreation of children, children are usually begotten in marriage, husband and wife cohabit for this purpose, the wife is assumed to have exercised relations exclusively with the husband after the marriage ceremony, father and mother provide for their own offspring.

A deviation from these ordinary assumptions and usual course of events would lead to confusion. Fathers would not be known, women alone would be burdened with children, the children would have no one to provide for them, the race would not propagate successfully, confusion would be rampant within society and the state.

The chief concern in establishing paternity is its effects of legitimacy and the right of succession. Illegitimacy, while it has been mitigated in the Code by legitimation, has limitations.[2]

[2] Canons 504; 232, § 2, 1°; 331, § 1, 1°.

In matters of inheritance the rights of the child must be safeguarded by legal provisions.

The "iustae nuptiae" mentioned in Canon 1115 § 1 signifies a valid marriage or one putatively valid. This is the so-called cause of paternity.[3]

Any marriage, then, that is *in possession* would indicate paternity, no matter how long or how short a time after the celebration of marriage a child is born. The underlying presumption in the law is that B, who is not with child, had conjugal relations with A, and that B was faithful to A from then until a child was born.[4]

To establish with moral certainty a possibility or probability of another father in a case is not sufficient. Canon 1115 § 1 insists upon evident proofs. According to the strict interpretation of § 2 of the same canon a child born in marriage could be reckoned illegitimate, *i. e.*, his legitimacy would be questionable if born outside the time limits there stated while the legal paternity could still be presumed. There is no contradiction here. Legitimacy could be *effected* as in Canon 1114. However, the time-limit provision in the Canon offers a husband an opportunity on which to base his proofs to exclude his paternity.[5] The only conclusive argument that can demonstrate non-paternity is total absence of the copula within the time period of pregnancy in every particular case. In other words the impossibility of fatherhood must be proved once two people are married. Physical impotence, absence through war, imprisonment, shipwreck, or business, or evident arguments that would prove conclusively that the presumed father did not have marital relations with the mother in a period from conception to birth to warrant fatherhood would overthrow the presumption. This last situation could easily obtain in marriage contracted by proxy.

Adultery might be alleged and proved, it may be admitted on the part of either the man or the woman, even a sworn statement at the point of death of a dying woman that the child was adulterine (the adulterer so confessing) would not destroy the presumption of

[3] Canon 1114.

[4] Triebs, *Handbuch des Kanonischen Eherechts*, IV, 666.

[5] Cf. Vermeersch-Creusen, *Epitome*, II, p. 241; Gasparri, *De Matrimonio*, II, 195.

paternity if the provision of time is maintained.[6] The ultimate reason for such strength on the part of the law is because of the lack of certainty. Presumptions operate only in doubt. The secrecy of necessary actions preceding conception, the positive uncertainty of establishing the moment of conception and the duration of pregnancy, plus the added uncertainty of discovering the father when any multiplicity of (at least two) men is admitted, all favor rather than destroy the presumption of paternity. As long as a doubt persists and no conclusive evidence is offered the presumption will be maintained. It yields only to truth.

Arguments derived from the approximate time of pregnancy by estimating the maturity of the child at the time of birth would not produce certainty in every case, neither would the differences of features, form, or even color. Should allegation be made on the difference of race a further proof would be necessary to show the lack of these qualities, *e. g.*, of color in the father or mother before the non-paternity would enjoy absolute certainty.[7] Blood tests, at present, while they assist in determining paternity do not prove definitely. It may be demonstrated that C, the child, has the type blood that could have been produced by A, the father, but this does not eliminate the possibility of another man with the same type as A of being the father, also. If the typing shows that A could not have produced the type blood possessed by the child, C, then A would be excluded as the father. In so far as the Church has not committed herself to any statement on this manner of determining paternity it cannot be said that She has endorsed this means of proof. *Ex silentio* it might be concluded that She does not accept it as conclusive. It is admitted that this is an indirect attack on the presumption of fatherhood, but

[6] Canon 1791, § 1. Unius testis depositio plenam fidem non facit, nisi sit testis qualificatus qui deponat de rebus ex officio gestis.

Cf. D. 22, 3, 29, 1: "Mulier gravida repudiata, filium enixa absente marito ut spurium in actis professa est; quaesitum est, an is in potestate patris sit, et matre intestata mortua iussu eius hereditatem matris adire possit, nec obsit professio a matre irata facta? Respondit, veritati locum superfore."

Cf. S. R. Rotae Decisiones, II (1910), p. 99-100. The praesumptio iuris et de iure indicated here no more obtains since this decision was given before the Code.

[7] E contra, Triebs, *Handbuch des Kanonischen Eherechts,* IV, 666.

it is only a negative argument. It would strengthen the argument of exclusion, also negative, mentioned previously.[8]

Because legitimacy connotes paternity 1115 § 2 is no more than a qualification of § 1. The legal method of establishing legitimacy and legitimation is given in 1114 and 1116. To settle doubts and to repel any attacks on the genuine fatherhood of a child the Canon states that a child is legitimate if born six months after the day of contracting a marriage. Accusations of having sinned before marriage could not be founded on the strength of this fact alone. Neither can the husband accuse the wife of unfaithfulness or repudiate the child she bears if born within this time limit. In the words of the Canon the child is legitimate. The important juridical effect for the child is that it can point to a valid marriage, a father known by law, a faithful mother, and demand all the effects that flow from legitimacy even if it be born prematurely or posthumously until the contrary is established.

There is, also, added protection for the husband against injustice and deception should a child be born into his household for which he is not responsible before the law. There is protection, too, for the mother and child in cases of desertion where by the arm of the law the right to support and succession can be claimed when the contrary, *i. e.*, non-paternity can not be established.

The appearance of a child in a family later than ten months after dissolution of conjugal life would be convincing evidence for separation *a mensa et toro* in a charge of unfaithfulness of the wife.

While the law does not so state, but readily provides, a further deduction for illegitimacy may be inferred if the husband after being absent for ten months returns to continue cohabitation only to find that before 180 days have elapsed a child is born. An immediate denial and proof of his absence would conclusively demonstrate that he is not the father. While such a child would be born apparently "ex matrimonio valido" (Canon 1114) in the face of the argument of non-copulation it would not be legitimate. This would subvert the presumption of legitimacy that is established in Canon 1115 § 2.

In regard to foundlings they may be presumed legitimate till the

[8] Cf. Triebs, *Handbuch des Kanonischen Eherechts,* IV, p. 663; Deutsche medizinische Wochenschrift, (1931), p. 723 sqq.

truth is known. While there is a strong natural presumption against them, that parents do not expose but retain and provide for their offspring, nevertheless for fear that any injustice be done to a few legitimately born, "odia restringi, et favores convenit ampliari." [9]

[9] Cf. R. J. in VI°, #15. Gasparri, *De Matrimonio,* II, p. 196; Benedict XIV, in Epistola *"Redditae Nobis,"* Dec. 5, 1744, § 4, "Cum vero hactenus, ut scribis, incertum sit, quo tempore filius ille vivens conceptus, quove in lucem editus fuerit, solumque constet de morte prioris Uxoris, et de secundo cum altera Muliere matrimonio: supervacaneum, extraneumque remanet examen praefatae controversiae, an, ad effectum legitimationis prolis, tempus nativitatis dumtaxat, an etiam tempus conceptus attendi debeat. Sed in his facti circumstantiis, quum certum sit matrimonium inter illius Parentes rite contractum, incertum vero tempus, quo filius idem conceptus, et in lucem editus fuit; si nostrum de eo iudicium exquireretur, filium hunc legitimum censeremus, quum Iudex in dubio debeat in bonum et commoda prolis propensus esse."—*Fontes* 350.

BIBLIOGRAPHY

Sources

Acta Apostolicae Sedis, Rome, 1909–

Acta et Decreta Sacrorum Conciliorum Recentiorum (Collectio Lacensis), 7 vols., Friburgi Brisgoviae, 1870-90.

Acta Sanctae Sedis, 41 vols., Rome, 1865–1908.

Biblia Sacra, Hetzenauer, P. Michael, 1914.

Canones et Decreta Sacrosancti Oecumenici et Generalis Concilii Tridentini, Vindabonae, 1867.

Codex Iuris Canonici, Rome, 1929.

Codicis Iuris Canonici Fontes, cura Emi. Petri Card. Gasparri editi, 6 vols., Rome, 1925–1933.

Codex Theodosianus, Ed. P. Krueger, Th. Mommsen, P. M. Meyer, 3 vols., Berlin, 1905.

Collectanea S. Congregationis de Propaganda Fide, 2 vols., Rome, 1907.

Corpus Iuris Civilis, 3 vols., Berlin, 1928–1929. Vol. I: *Institutiones,* recognovit P. Krueger; *Digesta,* recognovit Th. Mommsen, retractavit P. Krueger; Vol. II: *Codex Iustinianus,* recognovit et retractavit P. Krueger; Vol. III: *Novellae,* recognovit R. Schoell, opus Schoelli morte interceptum absolvit G. Kroll.

Corpus Iuris Canonici, ed. Richter-Friedberg, 2 vols., Leipzig.

Concilii Plenarii Baltimorensis III, Acta et Decreta, Baltimorae, 1886.

Decretals D. Gregorii IX, una cum Glossis Restitutae, Rome, 1582.

Decretales Pseudo-Isidorianae, Hinchius, Paul, Leipzig, 1863.

Denziger, H.–Bannwart, C., *Enchiridion Symbolorum Definitionum et Declarationum de Rebus Fidei et Morum,* 14, 15 ed., Freiburg, 1922.

Harduin, Jean, *Acta Conciliorum et Epistolae Decretales ac Constitutiones Sumorum Pontificum,* 12 vols., Parisiis, 1715.

Liber Sextus Decretalium, una cum Clementinis et Extravagantibus earumque glossis restitutis, Rome, 1582.

Mansi, Joannes Dominicus, *Sacrorum Conciliorum Nova et Amplissima Collectio,* 53 vols., Paris, 1901–1927.

Migne, Jacques Paul, *Patrologia Graeca,* 161 vols., Paris, 1858–1864.

Migne, Jacques Paul, *Patrologia Latina,* 221 vols., Paris, 1847–1870.

Sanctae Romanae Rotae Decisiones seu Sententiae, Rome, 1909–1922.

Thesaurus Resolutionum Sacrae Congregationis Concilii, 167 vols., Romae, 1718–1908.

Reference Works

Amos, S., *The History and Principles of the Civil Law of Rome,* London, 1883.

Ayrinhac–Lydon, *Marriage Legislation in the New Code of Canon Law,* New York, 1932.

Bonfante, *Storia del diritto romano,* 2 vols., Milano, 1924.
Bouix, D., *Tractatus de Iudiciis Ecclesiasticis,* 2. ed., 2 vols., Paris, 1866.
Cappello, Felix M., *Summa Iuris Publici Ecclesiastici,* Rome, 1928.
Chelodi, Joannis, *Ius Matrimoniale,* 3 ed., Trent, 1921.
Cicero, *De Oratore,* Lib. ii, C. 49–50.
Cicognani, Hamletus, *Commentarium ad Librum I Codicis,* 2 vols., Rome, 1925.
Coronata, Matthaeus a, *De Processibus,* Rome, 1933.
De Angelis, Philippus, *Praelectiones Iuris Canonici,* 3 vols., Rome, 1878.
D'Angelo, S., *Jus Digestorum,* Tomus I, pars generalis, Romae, 1927.
Devoti, Joannis, *Institutionum Canonicarum,* Liege, 1860.
Donatuti, *Le Praesumptiones Juris in Diritto Romano,* Perugia, 1930.
Droste, Messmer, *Canonical Procedure in Disciplinary and Criminal Cases of Clerics,* New York, 1887.
Ferraris, F. Lucius, *Prompta Bibliotheca Canonica,* 9 vols., Rome, 1885–1892.
Ferrini, Contardo, *Pandette,* Romae, 1927.
Freisen, Joseph, *Geschichte des Canonischen Eherechts,* Paderborn, 1893.
Gasparri, Petrus, *De Matrimonio,* 2 vols. Rome, 1932.
Gneist, Rudophus, *Instituionum et Regularum Juris Romani Syntagma,* Lipsiae, 1858.
Gregory, Donald J., *The Pauline Privilege,* Washington, 1931.
Heiner, F.–Wynen, A., *De Processu Criminali Ecclesiastico,* Ratisbon, 1912.
Hinchius, Paul, *System des Katholischen Kirchenrechts,* 2 vols., Berlin, 1869.
Kaas, Ludwig, *Kriegsverschollenheit und Wiederverheiratung,* Poderborn, 1919.
Knecht, August von: *Handbuch des Katholischen Eherechts,* Freiburg im Preisgau, 1926.
Lanier, Chanoine Henri, *Guide Pratique de la Procédure Matrimoniale,* Paris, 1927.
Lega, Michael, *De Iudiciis Ecclesiasticis,* 2 vols., Rome, 1896.
Maasen, F., *Geschichte der Quellen und der Literatur des Canonischen Rechts,* Gratz, 1871.
Maroto, Philippus, *Institutiones Iuris Canonici,* 2 vols., Rome, 1921.
Michiels, Gommarus, *Normae Generales Iuris Canonici,* 2 vols., Lublin, 1929.
Mommsen, Th., *Le Droit Penal Romain,* trans. J. Duquesne, Vol. I, Paris, 1907.
Muniz, T., *Procedimientos Eclesiasticos,* 3 vols., Seville, 1930.
Noldin–Schmitt, *Summa Theologiae Moralis,* 3 vols., Oeniponte, 1929.
Noval, Josephus, *De Processibus,* Rome, Vol. I, 1920; Vol. II, 1932.
Pirhing, Enricus, *Ius Canonicum in V Libros Decretalium,* 4 vols., Venice, 1759.
Pruemmer, Dominicus, *Manuale Iuris Canonici,* Freiburg, 1927.
Reiffenstuel, Anacletus, *Ius Canonicum Universum,* 4 vols., Antwerp, 1743.
Ricobono, Salvator, *Fontes Juris Romani Antejustiniani,* Florentiae, 1909.
Roberti, Franciscus, *De Processibus,* 2 vols., Rome, 1926.
Sanchez, Thomas, S. J., *De Sancto Matrimonii Sacramento Disputationum,* Ventiis, 1693.
Sanchez, Thomas, *De Sancto Matrimonii Sacramento,* Lyons, 1669.

Schmalzgrueber, Franciscus, *Ius Ecclesiasticum Universum,* 6 vols., Rome, 1843–1845.

Sherman, Charles Phineas, *Roman Law in the Modern World,* 2 ed., 3 vols., New Haven, 1922.

Smith, S. B., *Elements of Ecclesiastical Law,* 3 vols., New York, 1882.

Sohm, Rudolph, *The Institutes of Roman Law,* trans, James C. Ledlie, 3 ed., Oxford, 1926.

Tanquerey, Ad., *Synopsis Theologiae Dogmaticae,* 19 ed., 3 vols., Tornaci, 1922.

Thomas Aquinas, *Omnia Opera,* 25 vols., Parma, 1867.

Triebs, Franz von, *Praktisches Handbuch des geltenden Kanonischen Eherechts,* 4 Teile, Breslau, 1925.

Ursprung, W., *Verschollenheits—und Todeserklaerung* (AARAU), 1918.

Vermeersch, A.–Creusen, J., *Epitome Iuris Canonici,* 3 ed., 3 vols., Mechlin, 1923.

Vlaming, Th. M. *Praelectiones Iuris Matrimonii,* Bussum, 1919–1921.

Vromant, G., *De Matrimonio,* Louvain, 1931.

Wernz, F. X.–Vidal, Petrus, *De Processibus,* Rome, 1928.

Wernz, Franciscus X., *Ius Decretalium,* 6 vols., 2 ed., Rome, 1905–1913.

Wernz, F. X.–Vidal, Petrus, *Ius Matrimoniale,* 2 ed., Rome, 1928.

Westermarck, Edward, *The History of Human Marriage* (London, 1906).

PERIODICALS

Apollinaris, Rome, 1928–1934.

Archiv für Katholisches Kirchenrecht, 1857–1934.

Ius Pontificium, Rome, 1921–1934.

Theologisch, Praktische Quartalschrift (LQR), Linz, 1832.

Zeitschrift der Savigny Stiftung, Romanistische Abtei-Lung, Berlin.

Universitas Catholica Americae

WASHINGTON, D. C.

Facultas Juris Canonici

No. 94

1935

ALPHABETICAL INDEX

BIOGRAPHY.

John J. Manning was born June 1, 1900, in Newark, New Jersey. After graduating from St. Augustine's Parochial School in Newark in 1914 he entered the Pontifical College Josephinum at Columbus, Ohio, where he pursued the prescribed academic, college, and theological studies. On May 29, 1926, he was ordained to the priesthood and assigned to the Diocese of Buffalo. In the fall of 1932 he matriculated at the Catholic University of America for a graduate course in Canon Law. In academic work he received the degree of Bachelor of Arts from the Josephinum and in 1934 the degree of Licentiate in Canon Law from the Catholic University of America.

CANON LAW STUDIES

1. Freriks, Rev. Celestine A., C.PP.S., J.C.D., Religious Congregations in Their External Relations, 121 pp., 1916.
2. Galliher, Rev. Daniel M., O.P., J.C.D., Canonical Elections, 117 pp., 1917.
3. Borkowski, Rev. Aurelius L., O.F.M., De Confraternitatibus Ecclesiasticis, 136 pp., 1918.
4. Castillo, Rev. Cayo, J.C.D., Dissertacion Historico-canonica sobre la Potestad del Cabildo en Sede Vacante o Impedida del Vicario Capitular, 99 pp., 1919 (1918).
5. Kubelbeck, Rev. William J., S.T.B., J.C.D., The Sacred Penitentiaria and Its Relations to Faculties of Ordinaries and Priests, 129 pp., 1918.
6. Petrovits, Rev. Joseph J. C., S.T.D., J.C.D., The New Church Law on Matrimony, X-461 pp., 1919.
7. Hickey, Rev. John J., S.T.B., J.C.D., Irregularities and Simple Impediments in the New Code of Canon Law, 100 pp., 1920.
8. Klekotka, Rev. Peter J., S.T.B., J.C.D., Diocesan Consultors, 179 pp., 1920.
9. Wannenmacher, Rev. Francis, J.C.D., The Evidence in Ecclesiastical Procedure Affecting the Marriage Bond, 1920. (Not Printed.)
10. Golden, Rev. Henry Francis, J.C.D., Parochial Benefices in the New Code, IV-119 pp., 1921. (Printed 1925.)
11. Koudelka, Rev. Charles J., J.C.D., Pastors, Their Rights and Duties According to the New Code of Canon Law, 211 pp., 1921.
12. Melo, Rev. Antonius, O.F.M., J.C.D., De Exemptione Regularium, X-188 pp., 1921.
13. Schaaf, Rev. Valentine Theodore, O.F.M., S.T.B., J.C.D., The Cloister, X-180 pp., 1921.
14. Burke, Rev. Thomas Joseph, S.T.B., J.C.D., Competence in Ecclestical Tribunals, IV-117 pp., 1922.
15. Leech, Rev. George Leo, J.C.D., A Comparative Study of the Constitution "Apostolicae Sedis" and the "Codex Juris Canonici," 179 pp., 1922.
16. Motry, Rev. Hubert Louis, S.T.D., J.C.D., Diocesan Faculties According to the Code of Canon Law, II-167 pp., 1922.
17. Murphy, Rev. George Lawrence, J.C.D., Delinquencies and Penalties in the Administration and the Reception of the Sacraments, IV-121 pp., 1923.
18. O'Reilly, Rev. John Anthony, S.T.B., J.C.D., Ecclesiastical Sepulture in the New Code of Canon Law, II-129 pp., 1923.
19. Michalicka, Rev. Wenceslas Cyrill, O.S.B., J.C.D., Judicial Procedure in Dismissal of Clerical Exempt Religious, 107 pp., 1923.

20. Dargin, Rev. Edward Vincent, S.T.B., J.C.D., Reserved Cases According to the Code of Canon Law, IV-103 pp., 1924.
21. Godfrey, Rev. John A., S.T.B., J.C.D., The Right of Patronage According to the Code of Canon Law, 153 pp., 1924.
22. Hagedorn, Rev. Francis Edward, J.C.D., General Legislation on Indulgences, II-154 pp., 1924.
23. King, Rev. James Ignatius, J.C.D., The Administration of the Sacraments to Dying Non-Catholics, V-141 pp., 1924.
24. Winslow, Rev. Rev. Francis Joseph, A.F.M., J.C.D., Vicars and Prefects Apostolic, IV-149 pp., 1924.
25. Correa, Rev. Jose Servelion, S.T.L., J.C.D., La Potestad Legislativa de la Iglesia Católica, IV-127 pp., 1925.
26. Dugan, Rev. Henry Francis, M.A., J.C.D., The Judiciary Department of the Diocesan Curia, 87 pp., 1925.
27. Keller, Rev. Charles Frederick, S.T.B., J.C.D., Mass Stipends, 167 pp., 1925.
28. Paschang, Rev. John Linus, J.C.D., The Sacramentals According to the Code of Canon Law, 129 pp., 1925.
29. Piontek, Rev. Cyrillus, O.F.M., S.T.B., J.C.D., De Indulto Exclaustrationis necnon Saecularizationis, XIII-289 pp., 1925.
30. Kearney, Rev. Richard Joseph, S.T.B., J.C.D., Sponsors at Baptism According to the Code of Canon Law, IV-127 pp., 1925.
31. Bartlett, Rev. Chester Joseph, A.M., LL.B., J.C.D., The Tenure of Parochial Property in the United States of America, V-108 pp., 1926.
32. Kilker, Rev. Adrian Jerome, J.C.D., Extreme Unction, V-425 pp. 1926.
33. McCormick, Rev. Robert Emmett, J.C.D., Confessors of Religious, VIII-266 pp., 1926.
34. Miller, Rev. Newton Thomas, J.C.D., Founded Masses According to the Code of Canon Law, VII-93 pp., 1926.
35. Roelker, Rev. Edward G., S.T.D., J.C.D., Principles of Privilege According to the Code of Canon Law, XI-166 pp., 1926.
36. Bakalarczyk, Rev. Richardus, M.I.C., J.U.D., De Novitiatu, VIII-208 pp., 1927.
37. Pizzuti, Rev. Lawrence, O.F.M., J.U.L., De Parochis Religiosis, 1927. (Not Printed.)
38. Bliley, Rev. Nicholas Martin, O.S.B., J.C.D., Altars According to the Code of Canon Law, XIX-132 pp., 1927.
39. Brown, Brendan Francis, A.B., LL.M., J.U.D., The Canonical Juristic Personality with Special Reference to its Status in the United States of America, V-212 pp., 1927.
40. Cavanaugh, Rev. William Thomas, C.P., J.U.D., The Reservation of the Blessed Sacrament, VIII-101 pp., 1927.
41. Doheny, Rev. William J., C.S.C., A.B., J.U.D., Church Property: Modes of Acquisition, X-118 pp., 1927.

42. Feldhaus, Rev. Aloysius H., C.PP.S., J.C.D., Oratories, IX-141 pp., 1927.
43. Kelly, Rev. James Patrick, A.B., J.C.D., The Jurisdiction of the Simple Confessor, X-208 pp., 1927.
44. Neuberger, Rev. Nicholas J., J.C.D., Canon 6 or the Relation of the Codex Juris Canonici to the Preceding Legislation, V-95 pp., 1927.
45. O'Keeffe, Rev. Gerald Michael, J.C.D., Matrimonial Dispensations, Powers of Bishops, Priests, and Confessors, VIII-232 pp., 1927.
46. Quigley, Rev. Joseph, A.M., A.B., J.C.D., Condemned Societies, 139 pp., 1927.
47. Zaplotnik, Rev. Ioannes Leo, J.C.D., De Vicariis Foraneis, X-142 pp., 1927.
48. Duskie, Rev. John Aloysius, A.B., J.C.D., The Canonical Status of the Orientals in the United States, VIII-196 pp., 1928.
49. Hyland, Rev. Francis Edward, J.C.D., Excommunication, Its Nature, Historical Development and Effects, VIII-181 pp., 1928.
50. Reinmann, Rev. Gerald Joseph, O.M.C., J.C.D., The Third Order Secular of Saint Francis, 201 pp., 1928.
51. Schenk, Rev. Francis J., J.C.D., The Matrimonial Impediments of Mixed Religion and Disparity of Cult, XVI-318 pp., 1929.
52. Coady, Rev. John Joseph, S.T.D., J.U.D., A.M., The Appointment of Pastors, VIII-150 pp., 1929.
53. Kay, Rev. Thomas Henry, J.C.D., Competence in Matrimonial Procedure, VIII-164 pp., 1929.
54. Turner, Rev. Sidney Joseph, C.P., J.U.D., The Vow of Poverty, XLIX-217 pp., 1929.
55. Kearney, Rev. Raymond A., A.B., S.T.D., J.C.D., The Principles of Delegation, VII-149 pp., 1929.
56. Conran, Rev. Edward James, A.B., J.C.D., The Interdict, V-163 pp., 1930.
57. O'Neil, Rev. William H., J.C.D., Papal Rescripts of Favor, VII-218 pp., 1930.
58. Bastnagel, Rev. Clement Vincent, J.U.D., The Appointment of Parochial Adjutants and Assistants, XV-257 pp., 1930.
59. Ferry, Rev. William A., A.B., J.C.D., Stole Fees, X-107 pp., 1930.
60. Costello, Rev. John Michael, A.B., J.C.D., Domicile and Quasi-Domicile, VII-201 pp., 1930.
61. Kremer, Rev. Michael Nicholas, A.B., S.T.B., J.C.D., Church Support in the United States, VI-136 pp., 1930.
62. Angulo, Rev. Luis, C.M., J.C.D., Legislación de la Iglesia sobre la intención en la applicación de la Santa Misa, VII-104 pp., 1931.
63. Frey, Rev. Wolfgang Norbert, O.S.B., A.B., J.C.D., The Act of Religious Profession, VIII-174 pp., 1931.
64. Roberts, Rev. James Brendan, A.B., J.C.D., The Banns of Marriage, XIV-140 pp., 1931.

65. RYDER, REV. RAYMOND ALOYSIUS, A.B., J.C.D., Simony, IX-151 pp., 1931.
66. CAMPAGNA, REV. ANGELO, PH.D., J.U.D., Il Vicario Generale del Vescovo, VII-205 pp., 1931.
67. COX, REV. JOSEPH GODFREY, A.B., J.C.D., The Administration of Seminaries, VI-124 pp., 1931.
68. GREGORY, REV. DONALD J., J.U.D., The Pauline Privilege, XV-165 pp., 1931.
69. DONOHUE, REV. JOHN F., J.C.D., The Impediment of Crime, VIII-110 pp., 1931.
70. DOOLEY, REV. EUGENE A., O.M.I., J.C.D., Church Law on Sacred Relics, IX-143 pp., 1931.
71. ORTH, REV. CLEMENT RAYMOND, O.M.C., J.C.D., The Approbation of Religious Institutes, 171 pp., 1931.
72. PERNICONE, REV. JOSEPH M., A.B., J.C.D., The Ecclesiastical Prohibition of Books, XII-267 pp., 1932.
73. CLINTON, REV. CONNELL, A.B., J.C.D., The Paschal Precept, IX-108 pp., 1932.
74. DONNELLY, REV. FRANCIS B., A.M., S.T.L., J.C.D., The Diocesan Synod, VIII-125 pp., 1932.
75. TORRENTE, REV. CAMILO, C.M.F., J.C.D., Las Processiones Sagradas, V-145 pp., 1932.
76. MURPHY, REV. EDWIN J., C.PP.S., J.C.D., Suspension Ex Informata Conscientia, XI-122 pp., 1932.
77. MACKENZIE, REV. ERIC F., A.M., S.T.L., J.C.D., The Delict of Heresy in its Commission, Penalization, Absolution, VII-124 pp., 1932.
78. LYONS, REV. AVITUS E., S.T.B., J.C.D., The Collegiate Tribunal of First Instance, XI-147 pp., 1932.
79. CONNOLLY, REV. THOMAS A., J.C.D., Appeals, XI-195 pp., 1932.
80. SANGMEISTER, REV. JOSEPH V., A.B., J.C.D., Force and Fear as Precluding Matrimonial Consent, V-211 pp., 1932.
81. JAEGER, REV. LEO A., A.B., J.C.D., The Administration of Vacant and Quasi-Vacant Episcopal Sees in the United States, IX-229 pp. 1932.
82. RIMLINGER, REV. HERBERT T., J.C.D., Error Invalidating Matrimonial Consent, VII-79 pp., 1932.
83. BARRETT, Rev., John D. M., S.S., J.C.D., Comparative Study of the Third Plenary Council and the Code, IX-221 pp., 1932.
84. CARBERRY, REV. JOHN J., PH.D., S.T.D., J.C.L., The Juridical Form of Marriage, 1934.
85. DOLAN, REV. JOHN L., A.B., J.C.L., The Defensor Vinculi, 1934.
86. HANNAN, REV. JEROME D., A.M., S.T.D., LL.B., J.C.L., The Canon Law of Wills, 1934.
87. LEMIEUX, REV. LELISLE A., A.M., J.C.L., The Sentence in Ecclesiastical Procedure, 1934.

88. O'Rourke, Rev. James J., A.B., J.C.L., Parish Registers, 1934.
89. Timlin, Rev. Bartholomew, O.F.M., A.M., J.C.L., Conditional Matrimonial Consent, 1934.
90. Wahl, Rev. Francis X., A.B., J.C.L., The Matrimonial Impediments of Consanguinity and Affinity, 1934.
91. White, Rev. Robert J., A.B., LL.B., S.T.B., J.C.L., Canonical Ante-Nuptial Promises and the Civil Law, 1934.
92. Herrera, Rev. Anthony Parra, O.C.D., J.C.L., Legislacion Ecclesiastica sobre el Ayuno y la Abstinencia, 1935.
93. Kennedy, Rev. Edwin J., J.C.L., The Special Matrimonial Process in Cases of Evident Nullity, 1935.
94. Manning, Rev. John J., A.B., J.C.L., Presumptions of Law in Marriage Cases, 1935.
95. Moeder, Rev. John M., J.C.L., The Proper Bishop for Ordination and Dimissorial Letters, 1935.
96. O'Mara, Rev. William A., Canonical Causes for Matrimonial Dispensations, 1935.
97. Reilly, Rev. Peter, J.C.L., Residence of Pastors, 1935.
98. Smith, Rev. Mariner T., O.P., S.T.Lr., J.C.L., The Penal Law for Religious, 1935.
99. Whalen, Rev. Donald W., A.M., J.C.L., The Value of Testimonial Evidence in Matrimonial Procedure, 1935.

www.ingramcontent.com/pod-product-compliance
Lightning Source LLC
LaVergne TN
LVHW050203080826
844660LV00012B/342